A TRUE STORY

MOTHER
HAD A
SECRET

LEARNING TO LOVE MY MOTHER
& HER MULTIPLE PERSONALITIES

Stacey—

I cannot tell you how
much I love you for
all you do and for
who you are.

All my love,

A True Story

MOTHER HAD A SECRET

LEARNING TO LOVE MY MOTHER
& HER MULTIPLE PERSONALITIES

TIFFANY FLETCHER

Covenant Communications, Inc.

Published by Covenant Communications, Inc.
American Fork, Utah

Printed in the United States of America
First Printing: September 2010

16 15 14 13 12 11 10   10 9 8 7 6 5 4 3 2 1

ISBN-13: 978-1-60861-058-7

For all those who suffer in silence.
May you finally find courage to speak.

$\mathcal{A}$CKNOWLEDGMENTS

First, and most importantly, I want to thank my incredible husband, Sean, for his selfless love and sacrifice so that I could share my story with others. He is as instrumental to the writing of this book as I am, and without him my story would not have been told. His encouragement and support have brought me to where I am today, and I am a better person because of him. He knows me better than I know myself, and he is a man like no other. I cannot thank him enough for all he has done for me. He is my shelter in the storm, my beacon in the darkness, and my safety against the battles that rage within me. He loved me when I could not love myself and taught me, through example, that real love—the kind that lasts forever—can only be achieved when we are willing to sacrifice all we have for the happiness of another. I love you, Sean.

I would like to thank my agents, Peggy Keller and Ellen Kleiner of Blessingway, who believed in me from the very first time they heard my story. Their insights and advice were an essential part to making this book what it is today. They helped me take a very rough draft and make it into a beautiful story of love and forgiveness—one that my mother would have been proud of. They have become trusted friends and true mentors, and I will be indebted to them forever.

I want to thank my family for their support and encouragement through this process. It is difficult for all of us to discuss our past, but they were so willing to answer my questions and share with me the memories that we have tried so hard to forget. I am grateful to my father, George, for his determination to never give up, and to my stepmother, Cheryl, for helping my father find happiness again. I am very thankful for my siblings: Lydia for her spirituality and for her courage to walk a difficult path, Tammy for her cheerfulness and her listening ear, Blain for his ability to lead and his dedication to family, Christopher for his caring attitude and strong desire to serve others, and Heidi for her ability to love and accept everyone no matter who they are or where they come from. Were it not for all of you, I would never have survived.

I would like to thank my editor, Kirk Shaw; my publicist, Kelly Smurthwaite; and all those at Covenant who spent tireless hours preparing this book for publication. I would especially like to thank Kathy Jenkins, who was willing to talk to a stranger at a writing conference and accept my manuscript for review.

Thank you to those friends who read the early versions of the manuscript: Joy, Stephanie, Liz, Chuck Fife, and others whose comments and insights were invaluable to the writing of this book.

I would most definitely like to thank my children, Cayden, Braxton, Makenna, Jocelyn, and Annika, for giving up their mommy time so that I could spend the time necessary to complete this project. And for loving me despite my many parenting flaws. I love you guys!

Finally, I want to thank my Heavenly Father and my Savior for allowing me to feel Their love in the most difficult of circumstances and for never leaving me alone.

And last, but certainly not least, I would like to thank my mother for teaching me the true meaning of love and forgiveness. May she rest in peace knowing that her sacrifice will never be forgotten. She will dwell forever in our hearts.

AUTHOR'S NOTE

My mother was originally diagnosed with multiple personality disorder in March 1994. Later that year, however, the American Psychiatric Association changed the name from multiple personality disorder (MPD) to dissociative identity disorder (DID). The change was made to reflect the medical understanding of the disorder, as it is not a personality disorder at all but rather dissociation from reality. Although my mother's original diagnosis was MPD, I have used the more current term DID to promote the name change and the professional understanding of the illness.

CHAPTER 1
FAMILY SECRETS

What happens in this house stays in this house. Although she was now dead, the words resounded in my mind as clearly as the day my mother said them. I hated the words for what they represented, a life of hidden suffering. While relatives and friends gathered outside the small bathroom of the funeral home, lining up to view my mother in her last repose, I stood looking at my reflection. My eyes were swollen and glistened with new tears. "They glistened like Tiffany diamonds," Mom would say. "That's why I named you Tiffany."

I stared at a small window at the far wall of the bathroom. *Twenty-four,* I thought. It was the number of panes in the window. I had an incessant need to count things ever since I was a child, which only grew worse as my nervousness increased. Whenever I was nervous I found myself counting things, not consciously. It was an involuntary habit like chewing on nails. My mother said she did the same thing when she was forced by her father to . . . I couldn't think of it. Instead, I splashed water in my face from the running tap in the sink I stood next to.

I looked back at the window, trying to refrain from counting any more of its symmetrical features. It was the only source of light in the dismal bathroom. It was about five feet off the ground, with just enough clearance to squeeze light through but not much room for a person, unless that person was desperate. I was certainly desperate. I wanted to run away and avoid what was to come.

I splashed more water on my face in a futile attempt to bring back my senses. What's wrong with me? I couldn't just leave my own mother's viewing. What would people think? That was the ultimate question—the question that kept us in our social lines of what was acceptable and right. Who would dare stray from the accepted norms when the neighbors were watching?

There was nothing I hated more about myself than the need to be perfect in the eyes of others. Although I often told myself that I didn't care what they thought, the truth was that my life was ruled by how I thought others viewed me. Like a harsh slave master, propriety kept a watchful eye over me, as it did over everyone. If I stepped out of line, it would crack its whip of ruthful public scorn, and I would file back to my proper place and once again take up the labor of maintaining the community facade.

Mom also tried to maintain that conformity despite her secret, a secret she insisted we preserve as well. The same secret that I now had the freedom to discard like an unsightly thing. Yet somehow I was not willing to toss it aside. Was it my duty as a daughter? Was it the pressures of family? Did I really care what they, outside the door, would say? I knew what their question would be. "How did Vickie die?" they would ask. What I did not know was the answer. I knew how she died, but would I tell them? Could I tell them?

I splashed more water on my face and glanced again at the window. *Maybe a running start would help,* I thought, amusingly.

"Tiffany," said a voice behind the door. It was my sister, Lydia. "Umm . . . one of your children needs a diaper change." She paused for a moment. "Oh, and Grandpa's here."

The words shook me to an awakened state of duty. I quickly wiped the mascara from under my eyes, took one last look at the mirror, and started for the door. I paused a moment and looked to the ceiling. "You have to help me with this, Father," I said. "I can't do this on my own, you know." There was no reply, but I knew He was listening, perhaps even cracking a smile.

I stepped outside to find Lydia standing, waiting. "Where is he?" I asked.

"In the outside foyer," she said.

"Duty calls," I said, mostly to myself.

Four feet from the door to the foyer, it happened—what I had been avoiding. Since I received the news that Mom had died, I had been preparing myself for this moment. Now that the moment was here, I was just as uncertain as I was before.

In the door stood an acquaintance from church, and although she was not a close friend, she came along with the rest of them to offer her support of the family and to pretend with us that this death was unforeseen.

"Tiffany," she said, "I'm so sorry." She put her hands on my shoulders and looked into my face. She mirrored my mourning expression and then embraced me. Pulling back, she asked, "How are you holding up?"

"We're getting by all right," I replied. I felt the need to talk on behalf of the whole family as if I represented their collective feeling.

"This came so suddenly. I couldn't believe it. When I heard, I . . ." A look of shock replaced her words as if she were miming the rest of the conversation.

"It was a surprise to all of us," I said. That was a lie. I promised myself I would not lie, but there it was, blatant and unobstructed. It fell out like all lies fall into a conversation. They were the fodder from which we had grown our deceptively perfect lives. I felt guilty that I had contributed to it. Shame stricken, I began to excuse myself when the question came, just as I had seen it in my head a thousand times.

"How did she die?" she asked. Her lips seemed to move synchronously with my thoughts. Though she spoke the words, I heard them more than with just my ears; I heard them with my heart, like steady precautionary beats.

I did not see Mom when she died, but I could imagine how it must have looked from the descriptions I had been told. She was kneeling by the edge of the bed, her head and arms sprawled across the blankets. The vision was horrific, like a gothic painter's depiction of the Saints lying prostrate before their God.

I looked at the woman and her expectant eyes. Her question was artificial like everything else at the funeral. She did not care how Mom died. She was testing me to see if I would divulge those indiscretions of my mother—if I would tell her secret. I smiled and said, "She died on her knees praying." And that was the truth.

CHAPTER 2
ACCIDENTAL DISCOVERY

I remember screeching. That is what everyone remembers of a car wreck. It is a horrid sound that pierces the ears and assaults the attentions of spectators who otherwise move fluidly through their daily activities. It is a surreal experience that unhinges the coherence of what is normal and suspends it for moments after the collision. Like most other spectators, I stood doing nothing, an outsider looking in, unable to interpret the event. Without the acknowledgment that I was a part of this intrusion, I would have remained an outside observer and nothing more, but fate would have it differently. God wanted it differently.

It was the spring of my senior year of high school. I had my first job working at a burger shop not far from the house. Though it wasn't the most glamorous of jobs, it was a source of money, and for me that meant a source of freedom. Just having something to occupy my time, other than home, was a nice reprieve from the usual responsibilities I took upon myself. It was an escape of sorts, or so I thought, but soon I would know there would be no escaping. Like always, my home life would crash into the rest of my life, leaving me to deal with the consequences. I would never be normal.

The comprehension that something was wrong came long before the collision. The car was moving much too fast, much too conspicuous. The sight of it was an irritation, like a sliver prickling the senses. My stomach tensed and heart beat faster. Though I was viewing the accident from behind the counter of the restaurant where I worked, I felt a part of the event as if I had been riding in the car. It was a sickening sensation of dread and fear.

As the cars approached each other, time seemed to stretch to fill every sensation that was about to erupt. First was the screeching, which quickly faded as the explosion of impact struck me like the beating of a snare drum and then the crumpling and whining of metal that had been compressed beyond its capacity to give. The metal folded into rough angles as shattered glass scattered across the road. The random shrieks of evasive cars poured out their last objections to the abhorrence. Then, a silence settled like the slow exhalation of breath. A few more beats of the heart, and time sped up again.

I gasped as the realization to breathe came back. I stood a few moments longer trying to realize what had just happened. My manager took action first, rushing to call the police while the rest of the patrons and I continued to flow around this minor interruption. A few customers glanced subtly at the accident, trying to satisfy their hungered curiosity while others gawked blatantly, feasting on every sensual enticement of the anomaly. The accident presented nothing more than a minor distraction that filled the otherwise stale conversations of the patrons with a new freshness.

"I just witnessed that accident," I said. "What should I do? Should I go out and tell the police what I saw?"

"No, there were plenty of witnesses," the manager replied. "They don't need you as much as we do. Your job is here. Just take the next order."

I nodded in agreement. Taking a few short breaths first, I then took the next order, but something still seemed out of place. Despite my attempts to focus on the customer, my eyes continued to wander to the scene of the accident. I had a clear view of the car wreck from the large bay window of the restaurant. My scattered attention had nothing to do with curiosity; it had to do with a feeling. In the back mechanisms of my mind, I was still processing the accident.

Something had triggered a thought that was now constraining my attention. I could no longer resist. I looked at the cars, which now rested some distance from each other. The police had arrived and were approaching both vehicles. One of the cars had a female passenger who seemed to be slightly dazed. It was then that I recognized what had been plaguing my thoughts. The feelings of the accident rushed back like a tsunami. The woman in the car was my mother.

"Stand back, miss. No one is allowed beyond the sidewalk," one of the police officers said.

"But that's my mom in the car," I said. I had rushed out the door, leaving the customer without his order. The thought that I might lose my job, which I had only just started a week prior, never crossed my mind. The sight of Mom replaced all other thoughts with a single imperative: I had to take care of her.

"You're her daughter?" he asked.

I nodded my head.

"She's not talking clearly. We can't understand what she's saying, something about your father. She has sustained some serious injuries, and we need to get her to the hospital, but she won't let us touch her. We think she might have a concussion."

"I can talk to her," I said. "I can get her out for you."

The officer looked at his partner, who was trying to coax Mom out of the car. He turned backed to me and asked, "Is she on any medications?"

This question alarmed me. "The doctors have prescribed her a lot of different medications," I said. "I am not exactly sure which prescription she has taken. If you let me talk to her, I can get her into the ambulance for you."

The officer directed me to the car where his partner was still trying to talk to Mom.

"Mom," I said, "Are you okay?"

"Tiffany," Mom said. Her voice was slow and lethargic. "What are you doing here?"

"I was at work, Mom. I saw you hit the car in front of you and came out to make sure you were okay."

"I was going somewhere," Mom said. "Your father's going to be mad. He's going to leave me. Please don't tell him about this. I don't want him to know." She was pleading like a scared child.

"Dad's not going to leave you, Mom. You just need to get checked to make sure you're okay," I said.

"No, I need to go. Your father's going to be mad at me." Mom pointed to the police officer standing beside the car. "He won't let me go. I told him I need to go, but he said I couldn't."

"Mom, he's just trying to help you. You can't go anywhere in this car. You were just in an accident, and you totaled it."

"I didn't. I was just going somewhere. Where was I going? I can't remember, but your father will be angry with me when he finds out."

"Mom, the police are trying to get you out of the car, and if you don't come, *they* are going to be mad at you." I tugged on her arm. She resisted. "Now, come on, before they get really angry," I pleaded.

"Why are they mad at me?" Mom asked. "Did I do something wrong?" Her speech was still slurred, her eyes glazed, her mouth gaping, and her face void of expression.

"Mom, you just need to listen to them. Okay?"

"Okay," Mom agreed. "I'll come, but your father's going to be angry."

By this time, Dad had arrived on the scene. Before my arrival, the police had called him at home.

"Vickie, what happened?" Dad asked. "Are you all right?"

"George, don't be mad, okay. They wouldn't let me go. I'm sorry. Please, don't be mad at me."

Dad reassured her that he wasn't mad, but Mom continued with her pleadings long after she was placed in the ambulance.

When she arrived at the hospital, blood tests had revealed elevated levels of narcotics, and her stomach was pumped. Mom's demeanor changed also, and she lashed out violently at the doctors. Because of her erratic behavior, she was admitted into the psychiatric and behavioral unit. After two days of evaluation she was discharged. I waited for Mom to be brought out, not knowing why this was happening and hating her for allowing it to happen.

"How could she?" I said.

"Now, let's not jump to conclusions," Dad said.

"How can you say that? You know this whole thing is her fault."

"Let's just wait and see what the doctors say." This was not like my father; he should be angry. He was a good man, but patience was the least of his virtues. He knew something he was not telling me. Why?

"Mr. Young?" An older woman in scrubs stood above my father, a clipboard in hand. "George Young?" she asked.

"Yes," my father replied. "That's me."

"You're Vickie's husband."

My father nodded.

"Vickie was admitted to the behavioral unit for psychiatric evaluation."

"Yes. They told us."

"I have some news about her condition."

"Is she all right?" I asked. Although I was angry, I was still concerned.

"Your mother is fine," the doctor said. "She sustained only a slight concussion."

"Why is she under psychiatric evaluation, then?" I demanded.

The doctor looked at my father, who was extremely calm given the circumstances. He knew why?

"What's going on, Dad?" I felt alone and confused.

My father nodded, and the doctor turned to me. She paused as if to collect her thoughts. "We believe your mother has dissociative identity disorder. She seems to be a classic case, although our diagnosis is somewhat preliminary."

"What do you mean?" I asked.

"When a person experiences severe trauma, there are several different ways the mind copes with it," the doctor explained. "In your mother's case, when she was forced to deal with the trauma of her father's continual molestation, her mind dissociated with reality and created a separate persona, or alter, who would deal with the trauma for her so that she didn't have to. For this reason it is called dissociative identity disorder. In the instance of her father's abuse, your mother dissociated from the situation, and Sam, a three-year-old boy, came into being. From that time forward, Sam was the one who faced the abuse and suffered through it."

I stood, saying nothing. The words revolved in my mind. Dissociative identity disorder. It seemed surreal. I had known about my grandfather sexually abusing my mother and that it had caused her irreparable trauma, but I had no idea how much. Mom often jumped from one mood to another erratically, like a flickering light. We thought she might be bipolar, but her mood swings were more than just the bounding between limitless depressions to heights of manic excitation. They were even more random and often contradictory.

Mom rarely remembered what she had done during the episodes and was often disoriented. At one moment she would be a loving caretaker, while at others she would become violent and angry. She often acted as a small child, requiring my sisters and me to take care of her. Though the diagnosis fit, it was still difficult to accept that she had different alters. The thought of each of these moods being a distinct person, or alter, seemed absurd.

"How many alters are there?" Dad asked.

"We are not sure of the number, but we know there are at least three: Sam, Bill, and Vickie, your wife. Our main concern right now is Bill. He is extremely violent, and we had to restrain him. We believe there are even more residing in her body, but Sam doesn't talk much, and all Bill does is make threats. We are sure that through extended psychotherapy, we can interview more of them, but it will take time to draw them out. That is the problem."

"What do you mean? What is the problem? Why can't you help her?" My father became agitated.

"Normally a person with a disorder like this one would undergo several months'—even years'—worth of evaluation and treatment," the doctor continued. "The diagnosis itself, and identifying the individual alters, could take several months. Unfortunately, your insurance will not cover it. If you would be willing to pay the—"

"I don't have that kind of money," my father said. "I'm just a mechanic. I'm working two jobs as it is."

"I'm sorry," the doctor said. She placed a hand on my father's shoulder. "Without further treatment, there is nothing more we can do. I am more than willing to work with you in getting her treatment. As I said, she is a classic case, and I would love to work with her and learn more about the disorder, but this will require funding."

"But what if I can't come up with the money?"

"I'm sorry, Mr. Young, but my hands are tied," the doctor said. "Without proper funding, I will not be able to treat her. I truly am sorry."

"Then what will we do?"

"The hospital has decided to release her into your care." She handed the clipboard to my father. "I will need you to sign these papers. By signing them, you acknowledge that I have talked to you about her condition." She began to walk away then paused. She looked at my father. "I really am sorry." The doctor left Dad and me sitting alone.

My father remained despondent, looking at the clipboard. While the news came as a shock to me, it was not completely unforeseen. I knew Mom was mentally ill. I just didn't have a name for it.

As a family, we had faced Mom's alters, even the violent one, many times. Though we did not call them by their names, we knew when they were there, like haunting specters lurking behind her eyes. We had dealt with Mom's problem for many years, but somehow giving them a name made them new and more foreboding to us. The question remained between my father and me: how were we going to take care of her?

I was angry, just angry. There was no meaning to my anger. It expanded until it filled everything, and with it came hate: hatred for my grandfather, the doctors, even my own father, but mostly toward my mother. Although this news changed my perception of her, I still could not keep myself from hating her. She was the object in which my anger took shape. I hated her and yet I cared for her. They were two opposing emotions struggling to sustain the same space within my heart.

I felt guilty for hating Mom now, in the face of her illness, but I could not help but blame her. In my head, I felt that somehow she had given up being a mother and had allowed this to happen to her. I believed that God gave everyone the option to choose to be or not to be who they were. Such an idea is easily accepted by many, but when we are confronted with those who fall outside of that perception, we are faced with a dilemma: do we blame them for being the way they are or do we accept the fact that sometimes things remain outside our control?

I already faced a world outside my control and needed the hope that somehow we all have control. I hated my mother for what she represented—helplessness and the possibility that every effort I made to change or control my own life might be worthless. Was I like her, just a creature of fate, unable to break the cycles that bound me to this existence?

As the nurse wheeled Mom out, I found no words to say to her.

"I'm sorry, George," Mom said. Her pleas of forgiveness were as a little child who had just broken her parents' favorite vase. "I won't do it again. Just don't make me stay here."

"You're not staying here any longer, Vickie," my father said. Though he seemed tired, he spoke lovingly.

"Are we going home?" she asked.

"Yes, Honey, we're going home."

She smiled. "Thank you. I really am sorry."

"It's okay. Let's just get you home."

"You're mad at me," she said. "You hate me, don't you?"

She often acted like this. I would learn later that my mother had many child alters. One of them was Vicki, a seven-year-old girl. She spelled her name without the "e" because she said she hated the "e" at the end and voiced her opinion every time she saw it. When Vicki came out, Mom acted like what Vicki was, a child. She was always very negative and constantly saying we hated her. With the exception of Bill, none of the alters bothered me more than Vicki. I hated her, like many of Mom's alters.

"We don't hate you, Mom," I lied. Though Mom had many alters, we called them all Mom, except for one, the violent one. He made sure we knew his name. He struck fear into our family, and for that reason we spoke little of him.

"Did the doctors talk to you, Vickie?" Dad asked.

"Yes. I don't like those doctors." She yawned. "I'm tired. Can we go home now? I want to go home."

"I have to sign some papers, then we can go," my father said. "Did the doctors tell you why they were keeping you here?"

"They said I was sick."

"Did they tell you what that sickness was?" my father asked.

She hesitated for a moment. "They said I had other people inside me," she said, "but I don't believe them."

"What do you mean, you don't believe them?" I asked.

Mom looked at me as if to be offended by my question. "I don't think they know what they're talking about," she said.

"They're doctors, Mom, I think they know what they're saying."

"Why are you upset with me?" she asked.

"You wrecked Lydia's car," I exclaimed. "Do you remember that?"

She looked at me confused. "You hate me," she said. She looked at my father. "You both hate me."

"We don't hate you," Dad said. He handed the clipboard to a nurse sitting at check-in, took the handles of the wheelchair, and directed Mom to the car.

I followed a distance away, still thinking of the doctor's words. They did not want to care for her. My father didn't even want to care for her. He would go back to working his two jobs, and then who would be left to care for her: my sisters and me—until my sisters left home. Then it would just be me who would take care of her. That was my job. That had always been my job.

CHAPTER 3
A CALL IN THE NIGHT

The phone rang during that time of night that is neither early morning nor late evening, an ambiguous limbo of time where most decent people are in bed. It woke my husband and me from our sleep. At first it was a distant ring, almost disregarded as a dream, but then it rang again, this time more pronounced and deliberate as if the urgency of it could not be ignored. My husband, Sean, sprang from the bed, mumbling a few curses about the absurdity of calling at that hour. I too was annoyed. Having two children under the age of three makes one irritated by such intrusions to slumber.

There was one last ring, abruptly interrupted as if its life were being strangled out of it, then the gruff voice of my husband. "Yes, who is this?" he said. His voice still carried the same annoyed quality of his grumbling. He paused. "What's the matter?" he asked. Concern had overcome the annoyance in his tone.

A rush of thoughts entered my mind. Who would call at this hour? What could be the reason? Was someone in an accident? Is someone in the hospital? Then came the calming reminder that there was nothing to be worried about, followed by more of that naive reasoning the mind conjures up to protect us from unbearable situations. Still, in the back of my mind a thought lingered, the thought that came with each unexpected phone call. The same thought that had resided in the inner restraints of my mind when, in my youth, an ambulance would turn down our street while I walked home from school. What's happened to my mother?

A few more grunts of acknowledgment came from Sean, then the foreboding words, "I'll tell her." Sean clumsily hung up the receiver. His shadow could be seen contrasted against the long strip of light emanating from the hallway into our darkened room. His steps were labored and slow. He now stood at the door, and though only his silhouette could be seen, his expression was familiar. I sat up in bed as he spoke my name. "Tiffany," he said, "I have something to tell you." His voice was quavering as if the news he bore held an inexplicable weight, burrowing into his shoulders, inflicting unspeakable pain. He sat down on the bed and swung his arm around me as if he were scooping up a small child who had just been injured. I resisted him at first as if by not hearing the news, it would not be true. Then, with me in his embrace, he whispered into my ear, "Your mother is dead."

It was not the first time I had lost a loved one. That happened when I was four, and that news, too, came with a phone ring.

"Can we go with you to Grandma's today?" I asked my mother. I loved going to Grandma's house with my mother each day. We shared a duplex with my grandparents, and I loved the closeness that the proximity provided. Because of her illness, my grandmother was confined to a wheelchair and didn't go out much. Instead, she would sit in her oversized armchair while we cleaned her house and made her meals. When the chores were through, I would spend the rest of the day sitting on Grandma's lap or on the arm of the chair, and together we would share a can or two of Vienna sausages. Life was always better at Grandma's house.

"Please, Mommy, can I please go with you to Grandma's house today?" I asked again as my mother walked past me on the way to the phone. She did not answer me. My mother picked up the receiver.

"Yes. Who is this?" she said.

I pulled on her dress insistently. She looked down at me and then brushed my hand away.

"I'm sorry, could you say that again?" she said, "I didn't quite get that."

I puffed out my lip, crossed my arms, and stomped my feet. "Just a minute," she said. She placed her hand over the receiver and bent to talk to me. "Go play with your sister," she said. "Mommy's talking on the phone, and it's very important." She placed her hand on my shoulder and lovingly pushed me toward the living room. I shook her hand from my shoulder and stomped off into the other room. Lydia was there smirking at the display. I stuck my tongue out at her.

In the other room, I could still hear bits of my mother's conversation. "What about my mother?" she said. "Is she okay?"

I heard the receiver drop to the floor, and then my mother slumped onto the tile. She was crying. Lydia and I rushed into the room. "Are you okay, Mommy?" I asked. "Did you fall?"

She continued crying.

"I can kiss it better."

She smiled slightly. "Mommy's okay, Sweetheart," she said as she wiped tears from her cheeks.

"Can we go with you to Grandma's today?"

She looked at us with swollen eyes and a blank stare. "No, Grandma isn't home today. She has gone away and won't be coming back for a long time."

"Where did she go?" I asked.

"On a long trip," Mom answered as she bit her lower lip, trying not to show us she was crying.

"Grandma died, didn't she, Mommy?" Lydia asked. Even though Lydia was young, she could always understand things that were beyond her years.

Lydia knew that Grandma had died, and she understood death. She knew that death meant Grandma would not be coming home, but I could not understand it. I was angry that Grandma had left me without saying good-bye and that she would not be coming back. She was probably my best friend and my four-year-old mind couldn't understand the concept of death. I ran to the darkest corner of the house.

In the distance I could hear my father enter the room. "What's wrong?" he said. "Why are you crying?"

"She's dead, George," Mom replied.

"Who's dead? What are you talking about?" His voice was urgent.

"My mother." Mom broke out into more sobs. "It's my fault," she said. "I should have been there."

"How can you blame yourself?" Dad said. "She was ill. You knew this day would come eventually. It's not your fault."

"I was supposed to take care of her. It's my fault for not being there when she died."

I listened until I could bear it no longer. *Why would Mom say it was her fault that Grandma went away?* I thought. *Was it her fault?* I tucked my legs under my chin and cried. I said a prayer, trying to bargain with God. "I will be better, God," I said. "Just make Grandma come back. I promise I won't sit too close to the TV or pick my nose." Those were the only two things that Grandma ever got after me for. "Just bring her back, and I will never do anything wrong." I waited for a good long time, hoping for some answer.

My dad finally found me hiding in the corner and took me in his arms.

"What's wrong, Honey," he said. His voice grumbled softly.

"Grandma—she left us and isn't coming back," I said. "I want God to bring her back."

"Tiffany," he said, "Grandma hasn't really gone, you know."

"She hasn't?" I asked. I remember my heart felt a jump when he said this.

"She may be gone from her house, but she will always be right here, in your heart." Dad gently lifted my hand and put it to my heart.

"Will I ever see her again?" I asked.

"Oh yes," he said. "You will see her again. Grandma will be just like you remember her, only better, because her body will be perfect and she won't be sick anymore."

I smiled.

Grandma had been ill for as long as I could remember and possibly for as long as my mother knew her. My grandfather made it clear that it was Mom's job to care for my grandma. He even used her ill health as blackmail to keep my mother quiet about his indiscretions, saying it would kill her if she found out. Despite the sexual abuse that my mother underwent as a child, she remained close to her parents. Though she had a need to escape, she still felt tied by duty to care for my grandmother.

After Grandma's death, Mom was never the same. It was as if a part of her had died, the part that gave her purpose. Without her mother to care for, she had no reason to live near her parents' home. Mom and Dad soon decided to move to Wyoming. While they agreed this would be best for the entire family, I had different feelings.

"I won't go," I said, "and you can't make me." I stood steadfast in my determination to stay right where I was. I was always determined and stubborn.

"You will get in this car right now, young lady," my mother demanded.

"I'm not going to Wyoming. I hate Wyoming."

"How do you know you hate it? You've never been there."

"If it's not here, then I hate it."

"Get in the car!"

"No!"

Neighbors were now on their front porches watching the drama unfold. While this meant Mom was less willing to use abrupt force, it did not deter her entirely.

"This is not a discussion," she said. She pointed her finger at me and scowled menacingly. "You will get your butt in this car or—" Mom paused briefly to see who was watching "—or I will spank it." The threat was real. My mother was an extreme adherer to the philosophy of the rod, often using whatever instrument she had in her hand. She'd broken two wooden spoons and a hairbrush over my backside. Still, she didn't have an audience then. This knowledge emboldened me. I stuck my tongue out at her.

"That's it," she exclaimed. With the determination of an enticed bull, she stormed the stairs to the porch and grabbed me by the arm. "You are coming and that's final," she said as she yanked me off my feet.

As soon as I touched ground again, I began resisting, but her grip held firm. My father, who had sat with his head buried in the steering wheel, reached and unlocked the back door. Mom pulled it open and forcefully shoved me into the car against my sisters, who had shot across the seat in anticipation of my arrival. She slammed the door shut with a loud iron clang. My father glanced at the neighbors who looked on with gaping mouths. He politely waved.

When Mom got in the car, she looked at me through the pull-down mirror in the sunshade. Her eyes bore down on me like judgments from God. She said, "What is with you today?" Her voice was exasperated by the exertion.

"I just don't want to go," I said.

"But why? Is it your friends? Because you'll make new . . ."

"It's not my friends."

"Then what?"

A brief silence engulfed the car as everyone listened expectantly.

"I—I just don't want to leave Grandma."

"We will visit her grave when we come back."

"I know."

"Then why are you so upset to leave?"

"If we move, how is Grandma going to find us when—when she comes back?"

Realization came like a wave over my parents' faces. They looked at each other with amusement. Dad shook his head as my mother turned to look at me. She pursed her lips as she tried to keep a straight face. She said, "Sweetheart, Grandma will still be able to find us."

"But how?" I asked.

My mother chased back a giggle. "I'm sure Heavenly Father will tell her where we've gone." With that my mother turned around. She glanced once more at my father, and together they laughed.

I, on the other hand, saw no amusement in the matter, and the fact that my parents did upset me. I spent the entire trip with my arms crossed, speaking to no one.

To this day, I still retain fond memories of sitting on Grandma's lap eating Vienna sausages. She was kind to me and gave me the attention I craved. Now that I am older I understand death better, but I still wait for her.

"This can't be," I said. "There has to be a mistake. Are you sure they said she was dead?"

Sean nodded, his face carrying a somber expression.

"No. I don't believe it. Where's the phone? I'll call my brother. She's probably just gone to the hospital or something. There's been a mistake." I stood up from the bed and stumbled for the phone. I dialed the numbers and waited. In my heart, I prayed that it was just a misunderstanding. *Please, just let him be wrong—let her be alive.* I pleaded. *I'll do anything. I'll be better. God, just make it right.* A click sounded on the other end, then my brother's voice. "Hello?" he said.

"Chris, it's Tiffany. Is it true? Is she . . ."

"She's dead, Tiffany."

"But that can't be. She just celebrated her thirty-first anniversary with Dad." My mind swirled, searching for something to reach out to and to make sense of things again. "How—how did . . ." No. I did not want to know the answer to that now. "Are you sure?"

"Tiffany, I was there. I saw her body at the side of the bed."

"Was Dad there? Did he see?"

"He's the one that called me in." Chris hesitated as if the memory was causing pain. "He kept asking me to do something, but I didn't know what to do. I called 911. They told me to do CPR."

"Did you?"

"Of course I did. I did everything I could. I thought maybe I could bring her back, but when I started . . . I heard her sternum crack and her chest crumple under my weight. I felt like I was hurting her. She was dead and I knew it, but I had to keep trying to save her. I thought if I didn't do all I could, I would never forgive myself."

"I know you did all you could."

"My arms were so tired, but I kept trying to bring her back," he said. I had never heard my brother so emotional. "The paramedics finally came. They pronounced her dead and took her away."

There was a pause between the two of us.

"I should have been there. I could have stopped her."

"Tiffany, I was here. There was nothing anyone could have done."

I said nothing.

"How are you holding up?" he said. "Is Sean there?"

"Yes. He's the one that gave me the news. I—I just needed to hear it for myself. How is Dad taking it?"

"Pretty bad. But Tammy and Jeremy are with him. They'll take care of him." He hesitated slightly as if something was drawing his attention. "I better go. The police are here, they're taking down the report." He hung up.

I stood frozen, a cold breeze drifting into the room from the window. A storm was coming. I placed the phone down, wondering why I had not felt anything yet. I walked into the room and sat next to Sean. He looked at me, waiting. I was waiting too. It was silent.

"She—she's dead," I said. The words were cold and emotionless, but they struck me like a stake breaking through the frozen surface of tundra.

I placed my head on his shoulder. Over twenty years of anticipation had culminated into this singular moment, when the thoughts and worries that had plagued my childhood formed into the coagulation of an undeniable fact, as if those words, "she's dead," had blown a spirit of life into them that did not exist there before. Despite my denial, there existed no question of why or how. I knew what had claimed my mother.

Like a broken bridge collapsing beneath me, I was swept in the currents of emotion. My heart poured out eagerly as tears streamed. My cries came through exasperated gasps as if I were drowning beneath a heavy shroud of unrelenting agony. I gripped tightly to my husband, my head buried in his shirt wetted with my tears. He held me even more tightly, his tears mingling with mine. No words were exchanged; none were needed.

CHAPTER 4
TAKING CARE OF MOM

"Come on, Tiffany," Lydia said. "You're slowing us down. We have to get home." Although she was fifteen and I was fourteen, a little over a year apart, she still thought it necessary to take care of me.

"You're not my mother, Lydia."

"I'm not trying to be your mother," she said. "Who'd want to be?"

I ignored her, watching the children on the playground. It was a long walk from the school we attended to home. Along the way was the park. We walked past it every day, and every day there were the mothers with their children. I watched as one mother pushed her daughter on a swing. Both the mother and the child beamed brightly with the simple joy of being together. Why didn't I have memories of that? As a small child, my mother spent most of her time taking care of my grandmother. After Grandma's death, she didn't seem to take care of anything. She seemed dead herself, most of the time.

I watched as another child fell to the ground scraping his knee. The mother, concern in her face, sat with the child in her arms, gently swaying like tall grass in a gentle breeze. Soon the child's tear-smudged face was transformed to a gleaming smile as he looked up with tender love toward his mother. I continued walking, my heart swollen with a longing—a longing that I knew would never be realized.

"Did you hear what happened to Tammy?" she said. Lydia was never one for gossip, but she was always concerned with family matters. She was the one who never forgot a birthday and did everything she could to make sure it was special. She was kind. Although we were often at odds with each other, I loved her. She was my support.

"Yes, I heard," I said. "That Jessica is a snob."

"I can't believe she did that to Tammy," Lydia said. "No wonder she doesn't want to go to school."

We never had much money growing up, despite my father's best efforts to provide for us. As children, we often had to resort to hand-me-downs and clothes from the secondhand shop. For her birthday, Tammy had received a beautiful skirt that seemed almost new. She was very excited to wear it to school. That was until Jessica came along. It just happened that the skirt had once belonged to her. When she saw it on Tammy, she decided to take the opportunity for a little schoolyard ridicule. In front of all the other kids she confronted my sister about the skirt. Tammy of course denied it, but Jessica persisted. She pointed out a small rip in the skirt. "See, I told you it was my skirt," she said. "My mother sewed this hole after I ripped it on a fence." I could just imagine her smug little face when she said it. The thought angered me.

Tammy was devastated. She ran away as the other children pointed fingers and laughed.

"That—that . . . ugh." There were many things I wanted to call Jessica, but I couldn't. Mom always told us not to call people names, pointing to a verse in the Bible that spoke of not calling your brother a fool, even if he was one. Though I couldn't bring myself to call her some filthy name she deserved, at the time I found nothing wrong with resorting to violence. I guess I hadn't gotten to that part of the Bible yet. "I would have punched her lights out if I had been there," I said.

"Then it's a good thing you weren't there," Lydia said. She was always the practical one.

"She has the entire school saying we wear secondhands." I was furious just thinking about all the laughter and finger pointing we would get.

"We do wear secondhands."

"But no one has to know that."

"All I'm saying is that Tammy is still having a hard time about it."

"I know."

Lydia and I both bore the scars of ridicule. I myself had been teased about my weight, though I was the same size as the other children. When I fell off the monkey bars as a child, another little girl made the comment that I couldn't have been hurt, because my fat would have cushioned me. I wasn't fat at the time, and there was no reason for her to say it, but that is the way with childhood teasing: there is no reason to it. It isn't until we become adults that our teasing turns to more subtle forms of belittling, and we begin to attach reasons to it. Attaching reason to ridicule is like putting a bow on a knife blade before plunging it into the victim's gut in an attempt to make one feel less guilty of the offense. As adults, we may play different games than we did as children, but our cruelty never changes.

Lydia was especially sensitive to the teasing. When she was younger, her third-grade teacher had called our parents into her office to talk to them about her body odor. My mother took little care of us as children, and baths, among other things, were simply an afterthought for her. When Lydia found out that her teacher had called our parents in, she was mortified. From that day forward, she took on the role of looking after the younger siblings, making sure we had baths and that our clothes were clean. She wanted to make sure we did not suffer the same embarrassment she had.

We arrived at what was undeniably our house. In the midst of the ornately trimmed lawns and quaint flowerbeds of our community resided our home, a quarter acre of wild growth accented with spare automobile parts. Though it was March, the Christmas lights still hung haphazardly from the roof. Carcasses of several vehicles cluttered the driveway, where they had found their final resting place, monuments to my father's many unfinished projects. Dad's idea of upkeep was making sure our mess did not overflow into the neighbors' yards. Beyond that, the neighbors had to deal with the eyesore we called home.

I would like to say that the inside was better, but then I'd be lying. The inside was even more dismal. It was a disarray of dirty laundry, used dishes, and any other clutter one could imagine. Seeing it made the skin crawl and gave people the feeling of wanting to run away. After Grandma's death, Mom had stopped everything. It was as if she just quit being a wife, a housekeeper, a mother, even. She just quit life. My sisters and I had tried to take up some of the load of cleaning, but we soon became overwhelmed by the task. We quit too.

I opened the door. It was unlocked, as it always was. I don't know if it was even possible to lock it. Our philosophy was "who would want to steal from us?" Inside, I called for Mom. There was no answer. I called again but was interrupted by a sound from the kitchen. "Help," a voice called. It was Tammy. I glanced back at Lydia; her face showed the same grave concern as mine. We threw our bags down and ran into the kitchen.

On the floor, lying in a heap, were Mom and my sister Tammy, who was underneath. A hand waved from under the pile. "Help me," Tammy pleaded. We were not sure if Mom was passed out or dead. Urgency gripped us both. *God, please don't let her be dead*, I prayed silently.

Lydia and I each grabbed one of Mom's arms. Her body was limp and heavy. We strained to lift her. With great exertion we managed to drag her reluctant body off our sister. Tammy pulled herself up against a cupboard, breathing a sigh of relief. "Thank you," she said.

"How long has Mom been like this?" Lydia asked.

"About two hours, I suppose."

"You sat with her on top of you for two hours?" I said.

"Mom was cooking again, then she got dizzy. I begged her to sit down, but she insisted on baking cookies."

Cooking was a specialty of Linda, one of my mother's alters. At the time we knew nothing of our mother's mental illness. We only knew that my mother had strange and erratic behaviors that we called moods or episodes. After our mother's diagnosis and with the help of another of our mother's alters, Veronica, we were able to attribute names to these strange moods our mother had. Whenever Linda was dominant, there was nothing else on Mom's mind but cooking. She would cook even if no one was hungry and often in the middle of the night. We believe that Linda came into existence when our mother disassociated after the trauma of Grandma's death. Since Mom's greatest memories of Grandma were of them baking together, it seemed likely that this was the reason for Linda's incessant need to cook. It was as if she was cooking with my grandmother, though she had been dead for nearly ten years.

"How did she end up on the floor?" I asked.

"Like I said, she got dizzy and blacked out. She fell over. I tried to hold her up, but she just collapsed on top of me." I imagined our small twelve-year-old sister trying to keep our mother from collapsing onto the floor, her feet slowly slipping behind her as our mother's lifeless body lumbered overhead. Her feet would have been pushed out from under her, and she would have been flattened against the floor with Mom's body sandwiching her against the surface of the linoleum, trapped with no one around.

Lydia was standing over Mom, looking her over.

"Is she dead?" I asked.

"I think she's breathing," Lydia said, "but I can't be sure."

"Should we call 911?"

Lydia shrugged.

I put my face close to Mom's. I could feel a faint flow of air against my cheek. "She's breathing," I said.

"Maybe we should get her to her bed," Lydia said.

Although there were three of us, it would still be difficult to move Mom when she was unconscious. Even if we did manage to get her to bed, it did not remove the problem that she was unconscious and we did not know why.

"I still think we should call 911," I said.

"What about Dad?" Lydia asked.

"Dad's at work," I replied. "It will take too long for him to get here."

"Besides," Tammy added, "he might get mad, seeing Mom this way again."

"All right, call 911, then," Lydia said.

I reached for the phone and started to dial the numbers when my mother's moaning interrupted me. I put the phone away and huddled with my sisters next to her. She was slowly awakening, her movements sluggish and labored.

"Mom, are you okay?" Lydia asked.

Mom strained to raise her head, bobbing it erratically from side to side as if it were too heavy to lift. She looked up at us, her expression one of fear. She pushed us back with her arms and used her feet to back herself into the wall. She looked at us frantically but said nothing. She was like a scared animal.

"Mom, it's Tiffany. Do you know where you are?"

She continued to stare with no response.

"Do you know who I am?" I asked.

She nodded her head slightly. Though she recognized me, I was not sure if she recognized me as her daughter. Together with my sisters, I helped her into the bedroom. She was still in her nightgown.

"If Dad finds out, he's going to be mad," Tammy said. "He'll leave her. He'll leave us."

Tammy was always afraid that Dad would leave us. Her fears were not unwarranted. On one occasion, after an extremely heated argument, my dad burst out the door, yelling, "I can't take this anymore, Vickie, I'm leaving!" he said. Tammy was just a child, but she ran after him in her nightgown, grabbing his leg, begging him not to leave. I think the only reason Dad stayed that night or any night was because of that vision of Tammy, her small hands gripping tightly around his pant leg, her face with tearful eyes looking desperately at him while she spilled out plea after plea for him to stay.

"Dad's not going to leave us," I assured her.

"We can clean up the kitchen before he gets home," Lydia said.

I looked at Mom, her face smudged with batter and her gown dirty. "We can't just leave her looking like this," I said. "Why don't you and Tammy clean up the kitchen, and I'll take care of Mom." They agreed.

Though I was always angry for having to take care of my mother, at that moment I thought nothing of this. My only concern was Mom.

"I'm just going to clean you up now," I said. I grabbed a washrag and wet it. Mom cringed as I placed the washcloth to her cheek, as if expecting to be struck. I began to scrub the smudges with tender care, how I imagined a mother would do it. She seemed more frightened than submissive. In my mind, I saw her as a little child. Perhaps, in a way, I knew then what I know now—that it was not my mother but Sam I was caring for so lovingly.

Sam was always frightened and never talked much. We would find out later, from Veronica, Mom's alter who claimed to keep all of Mom's memories, that Sam was just one of the three children housed in my mother's body. When Veronica came out, we were able to talk to her about the alters and even found out their names. She said she could see each of the alters as if they existed bodily outside of Mom, waiting their turn to come out. Most of the alters did not use their names, except for Bill. He made sure we knew his name.

According to Veronica, Sam had blond hair and wore baggy pants and a torn sweatshirt. He was the son of Bill, who beat him continually. It was strange to have Veronica talk about these alters as if they were real people and not fragments of my mother's psyche. When an alter came out, Mom took on the persona fully. When Sam or one of the other children came out, she would adopt the mannerisms of a child. It was as if she was not my mother anymore, but someone else. Although, at the time, I did not know of Mom's alters, when she was in this helpless and childlike state, I found it easier to take care of her because I viewed her as a small child.

After washing Mom, I gently removed her nightgown, which was spotted with flour and batter. I gave her a shirt to put on, expecting that she would at least be able to perform this task. However, after several minutes of struggling with the buttons and mismatching every one of them, I decided to assist her. I undid the mess and buttoned them properly. She did not speak to me but only sat submissively, allowing me to clothe her. After dressing her, I rummaged through her nightstand for some earrings. "Would you like to wear some earrings?" I said. "How about these?" I presented her with a pair of loop earrings. She didn't say anything. She seemed frightened.

"You don't want them?" I said. My mother continued saying nothing, but by her expression I knew she did not want them. I put the earrings away.

Seeing that Mom was properly dressed, I decided to check on Lydia and Tammy. As I walked to the door of the bedroom, I heard a slight whimpering voice. It said, "Don't go." I turned to my mother to find her crying. I walked over to the bed and sat next to her.

"What's wrong?" I asked.

"I don't want you to leave," she said.

"I'm just going to help Tammy and Lydia with the kitchen."

"But if you go, you won't come back."

"What do you mean, I won't come back?"

My mother began to cry. I put my arms around her, and she submitted willingly to the embrace. "Don't cry, Mom. I'm not going to leave you. I love you."

I squeezed her tightly against me and began to sway. Though I was only fourteen, I felt as though I was responsible, not just for my younger siblings who, like me, were abandoned by my parents' neglect, but to my mother as well. I was responsible for her. I had to take care of her. It was a responsibility I shared with my sisters, a duty we would never be free of during my mother's lifetime.

I was angry that I had to care for my mother and siblings while others my age were celebrating their youth. Though at the moment, I would not admit that I hated Mom for it, I blamed her. She should be a better mother. She should be the one taking care of us. Despite the persistence of these feelings, I always remained loyal to my mother and family.

"Promise me you won't leave me," Mom said. She looked at me, tears streaking her face.

I smiled back at her. "I promise, Mom. I won't leave you." I held her tightly and began to sway again. "I will never leave you."

CHAPTER 5
THE TROUBLE WITH FUNERALS

The morning after Mom's death, the family met at the funeral home. We sat around a large oak table, which reflected the dimmed lights on its newly lacquered surface. The perfume of death hung uncomfortably in the air. No one spoke, out of fear. Fear that each word uttered would lead to that unwanted question of how. How did this happen? It always seems that such things are best left to be entombed in the crypts of deniability and rationalization. Yet each of us desired to know and thereby be relieved of the burden that comes from such secrecy. We looked to our father, who sat despondent and disconnected from the rest of us, his eyes stained red with tears.

The silence was contrasted by the memories of just a few days ago, when our family had gathered in remembrance of our mother. It was Sunday, and we had met at our parents' house for a celebration of Mother's Day. The atmosphere was jovial and light-hearted. Dad worked in the backyard, preparing the traditional Mother's Day barbecue. Mother's Day was one of the only times that I ever saw my father cook. It was his way of recognizing my mother. He was not a greatly articulate man, but his love for her was genuine, like a tarnished stone that glistened haphazardly in just the right light.

My siblings and I sat around the small dining room table jokingly complaining about how late dinner was. It was always late, and every gathering came off like it was pulled together on a moment's notice. Though this made for the occasional gripe, by me especially, it was the spirit of our family. The future was something that could take care of itself; these moments had to be appreciated then and there. Our lives were a string of these happy events scattered across a blackened shroud like stars escaping the night's darkness. Though the darkness may have seemed overwhelming, it remained as an accent of those moments of pure joy. It did not matter that dinner was late, at least not as far as recollection is concerned. What mattered was that we were together, and Mom was there and she was happy.

Now we sat again at a table, and Mom was not there, and we wondered, was she happy? It was the feeling that invaded all of our thoughts. Did she mean to leave us like this? After all these years, did she willfully abandon us? Such thoughts bring with it a tinge of anger and embitterment that must quickly be flushed away or it will fester and grow. The fact was, no one knew for certain the cause of my mother's death, and my father wouldn't allow us to discuss it. We had only speculations—speculations that could have been easily dissipated if we could have simply talked about it and broken the silence on the topic. But such silence is not easily broken and is often shattered like shards of glass that cut deeply. In the sight of so much pain, it is difficult to want to inflict more. So for our father's sake, we remained silent.

Instead we touched each other on the arm and made short consoling glances toward one another, as if our hands could speak and our eyes listen, but our lips remained still. The funeral home director stepped into the room and with him, a relief from the unrelenting silence. He was an elderly gentlemen wearing business attire. He greeted us with a warm yet subtle smile. In his line of work, one had to learn the art of contrasts. Death itself brings so many contradictions. Loving memories bring temporary happiness, followed by the anguish of loss. We speak of rest for our loved one, only to find unrest within ourselves. In unspeakable ways we hate them for leaving us in this vacant space while regretting not loving them more when they were here.

"Sorry to keep you waiting," the director said. His voice was soft with the appearance of concern, but it was evident that to him this was nothing more than routine business. "We will be going over the arrangements for the funeral. There is a lot to go through, and given the circumstances, whatever assistance the family can give will be of great relief to your father." He pulled out some papers and began thumbing through them before handing one to Dad. "We will need her information for the death certificate. Take this with you and fill it out. There is no hurry."

He then turned to the rest of the family. "Today we will be choosing a coffin and epitaph. You will need to make up a program and find flowers. We will be putting her obituary in three of the local papers. You can write the obituary yourself or we can use a generic form."

My siblings glanced toward me. They most likely expected me to write the obituary. I was the poet of the family who wrote such nice things, but how does one write anything nice about the death of a loved one? The thought embittered me. Yet to use the generic form seemed a betrayal to her memory. I would also be expected to give a eulogy, as if my words were a balm that could afford the family some healing from this absence in their life. Why did she have to die so suddenly? There was so much to do; when were we supposed to grieve?

"You may have the viewing here," the director continued. "We have a small chapel that should suit your needs if you wish to hold services there."

"We'll be holding the services at our church," Dad said.

We were a practicing Mormon family. Though at times during my youth we did not actively participate in church services, we always considered ourselves a part of the Church. In our later years many of my siblings, including myself, served as full-time missionaries. As my family joked when I was younger, one day we would stop practicing and actually go to church. My faith was the most important part of my life. It was the sustaining power that helped me through my darkest times. Now I needed it more than ever.

"Here, Dad, why don't you let me fill those out," Tammy said. Dad sat with his hand shaking as he tried to fill out the papers. Tammy squeezed his arm lovingly and pulled the papers aside. It was true, we had lost a mother, but he had lost a companion. We had our companions who stood around us with their warm grasps gently consoling us. He had no one now; he was alone.

The director smiled. "Shall we go and look at the coffins, then?" He stood up and showed us to the door. In the hallway, Lydia turned to me. "Tammy and I are going to dress Mom," she said. "We wanted to know if you were going to be there."

I hesitated to answer.

In the LDS faith, each adult member has clothing that they wear, whether it is undergarments under their regular clothes or regalia used in temple ceremonies. This clothing is considered very sacred and is treated as such. When a member dies, it is the duty of their children or close friends to prepare the body for burial by dressing them in this sacred clothing. In the case of my mother, it would be the duty of my sisters and me, her daughters, to prepare her body.

"You don't have to if it bothers you," Lydia said.

"No, not at all," I said. "Of course I will be there. She's my mother. I want to be there."

Lydia smiled and then hugged me. "I told Tammy you would do it."

"You thought I wouldn't?" I said.

"No. We just thought because of the whole thing with Uncle Elmer's funeral—you might not . . . you know."

"Don't worry about it. I'll be there." I acted injured, but in truth I wasn't sure if I would be able to either. The thought of seeing my mother's dead body and having to handle it made me uneasy.

Although Grandma was my first experience with death, I was not allowed to attend the funeral. Uncle Elmer, on the other hand, was my first funeral experience. I was six when he died after a short struggle with cancer. He lived with his wife, Bertha, whom we unaffectionately called "Bert," in a quaint little trailer house decorated with Coca-Cola memorabilia, which he collected from working at the plant. Unlike his wife, he was always kind to us, often bringing us bottles of soda or some other novelty from his work.

I was devastated to hear he had died. The last time I had seen him in life was in a hospital bed, his jovial face sunken and sickly. His bony shoulders had shown through transparent skin, and his once-wavy hair had been reduced to a barren skullcap. It was not the Uncle Elmer I knew. When I was told I would be going to his funeral, I was scared. If he were that distorted in his hospital bed, how would he look dead?

At the funeral Aunt Bertha was hysterical, claiming she was the next to go. She would be the next to go—long after her siblings had all died and her husband's corpse had decayed.

"I'm sorry for your loss," Mom said.

"He fought so hard," Aunt Bertha said. A distant gleam filled her eyes as if she were peering into the great beyond at her now dearly departed. "But alas . . ." She stopped abruptly and pulled a handkerchief to her quivering lips. A downpour of tears erupted as she placed her head on the shoulder of an acquaintance who seemed unsure whether he was a close enough acquaintance of the deceased to be lending his shoulder to his wife. "I'll be next," she said. "You just wait and see." She blew her nose on the handkerchief.

I was never very fond of old Bert. She was a cold, callous woman who had no use for children and thought they should know it. Bert was the one who told us that Santa Claus wasn't real. She saw my siblings and me as a strain on my parents and too much of a financial burden, but that's what she thought of all children. I always wondered what Uncle Elmer saw in her that would prompt him to want to marry her. I often imagined her with a shotgun at the marriage altar with Elmer tied up at her feet like a downed stag.

My mother and I walked to Uncle Elmer's open casket. I was not tall enough to peer inside, and this gave me some comfort. Still, I approached cautiously as if anticipating some decrepit zombie to jump out. I stood beside the casket, looking at my mother paying her last respects. She bent in and kissed the corpse. Thinking of her lips touching his decaying flesh disgusted me. My stomach churned. I was glad I couldn't see.

"Now it's your turn," Mom said. She was looking down at me, smiling.

"My turn for what?"

My mother smiled. "It's your turn to say good-bye." She then bent down and picked me up and helped me over the casket.

I closed my eyes, not wanting to see Uncle Elmer's decaying body. In my mind I saw worms and bugs crawling around and through his face.

"Come on now," Mom said. "Say good-bye."

"Good-bye," I said. I left no time for a reply, I wanted down.

"At least open your eyes when you say it."

I opened one eye and glanced down. To my surprise, Uncle Elmer's face looked better than it did in the hospital bed. The postmortem bloating had filled in his sunken cheeks, and the funeral home had graciously applied makeup to give him a more lively color. It seemed artificial. That is what I remember most about the funeral—it all seemed so artificial.

"Good—good-bye, Uncle Elmer," I said.

"That's better," Mom said. She smiled. "Now give him a kiss on the cheek."

I looked at her with a shocked expression. "Uhh-uhh."

"Come on. You always give your Uncle Elmer kisses on the cheek."

He's never been dead before, I thought.

"It will help you say good-bye," she said.

I looked at Elmer's stiff and lifeless face then back at my mother. I shook my head.

"Go ahead, Sweetheart. There's nothing wrong."

Seeing Mom would not relent on this, I conceded. Slowly I leaned forward as Mom lowered me toward the corpse. The smell of formaldehyde assaulted my nostrils and caused my head to swoon. She lowered me further. At this distance I could see the thick smears of peach makeup on his face. I closed my eyes and dove toward the cheek, plopping a quick one then craned back before any of a number of horrid things could happen to me. I wiped my mouth frantically as if it would fall off if I left any of Uncle Elmer's dead-people residue on it.

Mom let out that sigh that mothers do when they have been successful in getting their child to do something cute and distasteful. "We need to get a picture of that," she said. She swung me from side to side as she searched for someone with a camera. In the confusion, I managed to wrestle my way to the ground and bolt out the door.

I vowed then and there I would never go to another funeral again, a vow I kept until now. The thought of seeing my mother's dead body was unsettling, but I had no choice. This was one funeral I could not run from.

Together my family and I were led to a room adjoining the conference room we had been waiting in. It was lined with several caskets, like a tomb within a catacomb. The director began describing the differences in the caskets. Each was exquisitely lined with silk far more lavish than any bed Mom had experienced in life. It seems to be human nature to give the dead the greatest concessions in their burial, though little may have been given in life. We were a poor family with very little extravagances. Dad was a mechanic who often worked two or three jobs to provide. Although we had little, it had hardly been our greatest concern.

As we examined each of the caskets, conversations emerged as to which Mom would have liked best. We always thought we knew our mother, but knowing our mother was much more difficult than the acquaintance of one individual's tastes and desires. Our mother was a mix of several individuals, all with their own preferences and appetites. To say that my mother liked lilacs was to say that Vickie liked lilacs. To say that my mother liked cooking was to say that Linda liked cooking. Though each individual was different, each was literally part of my mother. The doctors may have termed her different facets as "alters," but this was just an impersonal labeling by those who knew nothing of our mother. We called each of them Mom.

Hate or love, they were all Mom. To hate them was to hate my mother. To love them was to love her too. Now she was dead—and they with her—to be buried in a single casket as they once dwelled in a single body.

That was her secret, sealed behind her closed lips to be engulfed in earth. I do not know whether she ever truly believed that the other alters existed. She knew nothing of them, except for what we told her, although they knew of Mom and her past. She denied for many years their existence despite the doctor's diagnosis. How does someone who has spent a lifetime in a house alone accept that she was never truly alone, but with a host of others? No one desires to acknowledge the fragile state of her own mind, and few are willing to take up the stigma of mental illness to be borne like a scarlet insignia in front of the world.

She was shunned for a sin that was not her own and an illness she could not cure herself. Seeing the pain she endured from such an unspeakable burden, it is difficult not to think that her passing was a relief to her. She deserved to rest, and we would give it to her with silken linens in the most beautiful of caskets.

"That one," my father said. He pointed to a washed lavender casket that glinted like chrome. Etched on the outside were roses like the ones Dad would bring home on those special occasions that seemed to stretch further apart as the years drew on. Inside was a single rose stitched into the lining. "Vickie would love it."

The funeral director made a note on his clipboard, saying nothing.

"Wait," I said. "How much is it?"

The director pulled up a tag from underneath and quoted the price: $4500.

I turned to my father. "Dad, that's too much."

"I don't care," he said.

"But how are you going to pay for it?"

"I have the insurance money. I'm getting ten thousand."

The funeral director made another note on his clipboard.

I stood closer to my father, trying to move our discussion from earshot of the director. "Dad, you could use that money to pay off some of your bills."

"I'll be fine." Dad could be stubborn, but so could I. Out of all my siblings, I was the one who could talk sense into my father when no one else could.

"Your mortgage payment is already three months behind," I said. "They'll foreclose on the house, then where will you be?"

"That doesn't matter right now. What matters is that your mother is properly buried."

"You're talking about her body, not Mom. She's not going to be in the ground, and I don't think she would want you to spend that much money on something she can't even appreciate, especially if it puts you out of a home."

"She is my wife, Tiffany. She deserves more."

Deserves more? I thought. *She wasn't even a mother to us. She's the reason we had no money growing up.*

I bit my lip, trying not to say something that would be regrettable later. "I'm just saying we need to consider where this money is going to come from."

"I told you, I have the insurance money."

"But we don't even know if you're going to get that money," I exclaimed.

Anger erupted in my father's face. He knew what I meant by the remark. Mom was found with an empty prescription bottle. Although the coroner had found high levels of medication in her system and ruled this the cause of death, they had not determined whether it was an accidental overdose or suicide. If it was suicide, my father would not receive a penny of the insurance money.

Dad was angry now. "I will get that casket and anything else I want, and that's the end of the discussion." He turned and walked to the director. Together they discussed what the vault should be.

Lydia, who had been overhearing the argument, put her arm around my shoulders and walked with me over to the casket. "You have to understand this is his wife who has died," she said.

"I know, but he needs that money," I said.

"You know Dad. Money means nothing to him."

"That's the problem," I said.

"If it were Sean, you would do the same thing," she said.

I said nothing.

"He needs this," Lydia added. "Let him have this."

"But what about . . ."

"It will be okay."

I looked at my father discussing the arrangements with the director. He was more animated than he had been before, as if a new sense of purpose had been discovered. In the end, purpose is far more valuable than any other commodity. In this moment of anguish, it was all there was to feast upon, like a treasure from the heavens.

I ran my hand over the silken lining of the casket, outlining each of the petals of the embroidered rose. I thought of Mom resting peacefully within it. We would bury her in the bosom of the earth where the torrents of sorrow could no longer reach her, and together we would pray that God would somehow relieve her of the suffering we could not. We would honor our mother and love her for all that she was.

Tears gathered at the corner of my eyes where they pooled together but moved no further. I quickly wiped them away.

We finished the arrangements and walked to the foyer, where the funeral director discussed the final preparations. My siblings filtered out, taking Dad with them. Before leaving, the director gave me the last of my mother's possessions that were with the body: her clothes and wedding ring. I stood alone holding my mother's things.

Chapter 6
It's Not My Mother

"Did your father ever abuse your mother?" the police officer asked.

"No," I exclaimed. "How can you ask that?" I was nineteen, standing in the waiting room of the ER, holding my mother's things. She had been admitted less than an hour before. My father was talking frantically to the nurses, trying to get an update about her condition. My father had a temper and often got angry with my mother, but abuse was a strong accusation. "My father loves her," I added as if I had to defend my claim.

"I know this is hard for you," the officer said, "but this information is important. The nurse said that you and your father brought your mother into the ER. Is that right?"

"Yes," I said.

The officer made a note on a small notepad.

"And you told the nurses that your mother had fallen down?"

"Yes. Look, I want to see my mother."

"In a moment. We need to get this report filled out. The nurse called the police because the injuries your mother sustained did not seem consistent with a fall. She's beat up pretty badly."

"But she did fall," I said. I was becoming agitated. "I knew I should not have left my mother alone, but I had to go in to work. I would only be a few hours at the most. She kept insisting that she needed dry mustard."

The officer looked confused. He started to write a note then hesitated. "Why don't you start from the beginning," the officer said.

"I'm late," I said. I was frantically searching through piles of clutter, looking for my keys. "I should have been there by now."

The house was always a disaster, but it was never as noticeable to me as when I had to find something. Growing up in such a condition had provided a certain degree of tolerance. What was repulsive to most was merely a distraction to me. Though I considered myself a perfectionist, I found that perfection was a relative thing. In the areas that mattered to me, I was meticulous and strived to maintain that aura of flawlessness. However, when it came to organization, I was less concerned. I had lived with disorder all my life, and my mind had learned to ignore it, perhaps in order to maintain a certain level of sanity. Our minds do that; they adapt and shape themselves in such a way that allows us to continue functioning in the most inhumane conditions.

"I need it for the deviled eggs," Mom said.

"Need what?" I asked. I was distracted by the task at hand.

"Dry mustard," she exclaimed.

I paused my search and looked at my mother. "Dry mustard?"

"For the deviled eggs." She was wielding a spatula caked with a mixture of egg yolk and mayo as if it was obvious what she was doing.

My mother often did peculiar things, so it was never evident what she was doing. When she became disoriented or if an alter came out, she would say many absurd things. Most of the time we entertained these eccentricities, often to our own amusement.

On one occasion, she insisted she had to dress the cats for the Queen's dinner. The oddity of this statement was only compounded by the fact that we had no cats. It was as if she was a small child playing a game and we would happily play along. However, these slight excursions from sanity did, on occasion, lead her into very dangerous situations. The act of making deviled eggs seemed harmless.

"I can't go to the store right now," I said. "I have to go to work."

"That's okay. I can get some from the neighbors."

"No," I exclaimed. "You stay here."

When Mom was in one of her states, we tried to make sure that she did not go out. Partly because of the scandalous looks she attracted from neighbors, but also for her own protection. At home she was safe enough, but outside it was impossible to know what could happen.

I lifted a pile of papers off the table, revealing my keys. I grabbed them and made for the door. Before leaving, I turned to my mother. "Mom, I will pick some up on the way home from the store," I said. "Just stay here until I get back. Can you do that?"

She hesitated. "But I can just . . ."

"I don't have time to argue about this," I said. "Please, just promise you will stay here."

She reluctantly agreed.

"Thank you," I said. "I won't be long. Just stay here until I get back."

I gave my mother a kiss on the cheek and ran out the door. As I got in the car to leave, a foreboding feeling came over me, a feeling that I should stay. I had always trusted in such feelings but was running late, and my job depended on my being there. Besides, if I stayed home every time my mother had an episode, I would be fired. "She isn't my responsibility," I said to myself. A sick feeling welled in the pit of my stomach, but I left anyway. I had to get to work. I was the manager; that was my responsibility.

At work my nerves had settled slightly, but I could not shake the feeling that something bad was going to happen. Although Mom agreed to stay home, she often did not keep such promises. It was not that she would purposely break her word. She was a very religious woman and felt strongly about such character traits as integrity and trustworthiness. However, her other alters

were either ignorant to her promises or simply did not hold the
same strict moral code. As a child, I often saw my mother as a liar
because of this. It was not until she was diagnosed that I realized
it might not have been her fault. Still, it was difficult to separate
the actions of her alters from those of my mother.

I began the meeting, discussing the benefits of working with
the corporation. Two new employees watched with that despondent flair for which soon-to-be teenage fry cooks were notorious.
The whole process of orientation seemed ridiculously irrelevant.
Most of the precautions in the safety video were at the level of
what should be common sense, but it seems the need for such
elementary knowledge was becoming more needed. For the
corporation, it was a necessity to avoid the much-too-prevalent
lawsuits. Despite their collective intelligence, which was hopefully
above that of a chimpanzee, they would be subjected to the ins
and outs of why putting your hand in a fry cooker was a bad idea.
As I looked into their glazed eyes and bewildered expressions, I
was not sure that this information would not be totally pointless
for them.

I turned on the informational safety video for them and went
to the phone to check on Mom. As I dialed the number and
waited, my stomach strained with each ring. *Come on, pick up,
Mom,* I thought. *Why isn't she picking up?* A number of scenarios
raced through my head, none of them good. Five rings sounded
now, and still no answer. With each ring the situation became
even more urgent, until my patience for the next ring became
unbearable, like a hope that was slowly being extinguished with
each of my exasperated breaths.

I slammed the phone down and grabbed a phone book.
Nervously, I search for the name of the neighbor. The words of
my mother played over in my mind like a relentless recording: *I'll
just go to the neighbor's.* I found the number and dialed anxiously.
One ring then two sounded. "Father, please let her be there," I

muttered. Though this seemed like an offhand comment, it was truly an attempt to implore God.

"Hello," my neighbor said on the other end.

"Yes, it's me, Tiffany. Is my mother . . ."

"Thank goodness it's you," she said. "I have been trying to get a hold of you."

"Why? What's wrong? Is it my mother?" I was stammering and incoherent in my words. The anticipation of what might be wrong was unraveling my calm like a string pulled from a loose stitch.

"I think you better come right now," she said. "I think your mother may need to go to the emergency room."

"What—what's wrong?"

"Just come quickly. I'm with your mother."

When I arrived at the neighbor's house, she showed me to Mom. "She came to my door looking like this," the neighbor said.

My mother's face was swollen and bloodstained. A gaping wound cut across her head, still seeping with blood, which trickled slowly down her face. The fleshy interior of the wound was riddled with bits of gravel and dirt. Her right eye had swelled to the size of a large fist. The entire side of her face was blackened from bruises. On her leg was another gash torn to the shin, oozing blood.

"What happened?" I exclaimed.

"I don't know," the neighbor said. "At first I thought she had come for help, but then she asked if she could have dry mustard. She seemed oblivious to the severity of her injuries. I think she may be in shock."

"But how did she get hurt so badly?"

"She just keeps saying that she fell," the neighbor said. "I can't get her to say anything more about it. I think she needs to go to the hospital."

"I'll take her," I said.

"Do you need me to go with you?" the neighbor asked.

"No. I can take it from here. I'll try to get a hold of my dad."

At home, I pulled my mother out of the car and helped her to the door. Along the path was a trail of blood. Inside, the trail continued to the bathroom where my mother had attempted to clean herself up before walking to the neighbor's. In the bathroom, blood canvassed the sink, floor, mirror, and walls like some horrific artwork.

I sat Mom on the couch before calling my father. I managed to catch him at work. He told me to wait for him to get there. As I waited, I tried to talk to Mom about what had happened to her.

"What happened to you?" I asked.

"I went to the neighbor's for dry mustard," she said.

"I told you to stay here," I said. "You promised me you would stay here."

She looked at me confused.

"You don't remember, do you?"

She continued to stare at me.

"Did you fall?" I asked.

"Yes," she said. "I was trying to fix my sandal, and I fell into the road." Although her words were strained, she had not yet shown any signs that she was even aware of pain. She was so beaten up, I could not understand how she was unable to feel anything. Perhaps it was the shock or perhaps something else.

"Did you take any medication?"

She did not answer. She had many medications from the doctors, some pain medication for a neck injury, antidepressants, hormone pills, and diet pills. It was evident that she had taken more medication than she should have, but it was never clear if she intended to do this. It was completely likely she had no idea how much medication she was taking. I imagined having alters was like several individuals each going about the same tasks without any knowledge of what the others were doing. Each would know she needed the medication, but none would know that the other had already taken it. Then again, there was the possibility that my mother did know and she was a liar. There was also the possibility that one or two of her alters had a drug addiction and Mom was a slave to it. There was no way of really knowing for sure.

Frustrated, I stormed into the bathroom and grabbed a wetted towel. I began washing her open wounds, trying to wipe the blood away. She did not cringe, didn't react in any way. It was as if she was completely numb. "It's just a little cut," she said.

"It's more than a little cut, Mom," I said. "Why didn't you call me?"

"I didn't want you to come home," she said. "You had to work."

"But, Mom, you've been bleeding really bad. You may have a concussion."

"I'm fine. It doesn't hurt."

My father burst through the door and immediately took hold of Mom. He pulled her from the couch and began taking her to the car. His grip seemed harsh, but his look was one of urgency. "We need to get her to the hospital," he demanded.

Suddenly, Mom jerked back as if a horrible realization came. She pulled away from my father. "I'm not going to the hospital," she said.

"Vickie, you have to go to the hospital," Dad said. His demeanor was gruff.

"I'm not going to the hospital." She pushed Dad away and stumbled toward the bedroom. "I won't go," she yelled.

Mom refused to go to hospitals after her experience of being held in the psychiatric ward. Whenever going to a hospital was mentioned, she violently refused.

"You have to be checked out by the doctors," Dad demanded.

"I'm not going," she said. She went to the bedroom and slammed the door.

Dad was angry. He started after her, but I stopped him. I was the one who could always calm my father when he was angry. We had an understanding that way. Growing up, I suffered my father's wrath more than anyone because of my stubbornness. Now that I was older, though, Dad respected my independent spirit. He would listen to me when no one else could get through to him. I held his arm, restraining him. "I'll talk to her," I said.

I opened the door to the bedroom. My mother was lying on her bed, curled into a ball. I sat beside her and stroked her hair. She looked up at me. "I'm not going to the hospital," she said.

"I know you don't want to go to the hospital," I said. "But don't you think we should have a doctor look at that cut on your head?"

"No," she exclaimed. "They'll think I'm crazy and keep me there."

"They'll just check you out, then you can come home."

"No. They'll keep me there."

It was clear there would be no convincing her that she should go to the hospital. I didn't want to lie to her, but there seemed no other way to get her the medical help she needed. I continued to stroke her hair.

"Well if you don't want to go to the hospital, maybe we could go for a ride," I said. "You like taking rides up in the mountains."

She looked at me but said nothing.

"Dad could come with us. You two could sit in the back while I drive."

I hated lying and tried to always be honest. I can think of only a few occasions that I may have lied as a child. In my mind there was nothing worse. Yet I found myself often having to pull at the truth. It was like a lie a parent would tell a child either to protect their fragile innocence or because the truth was too unsettling to them. My mother's eyes carried that childlike quality, like a child asking if Santa Claus was real. "No hospital?" she said.

The question tore at my heart. As I fought tears, I said, "No hospital."

I helped my father put her in the backseat. Dad rode in the back, holding her in his arms while I drove to the hospital. A few minutes later, we pulled up to the ER entrance. When my mother realized it was the hospital, she began to fight violently. We were able to get her into the ER with the help of a couple of interns. She continued to thrash about on the gurney as the doctors tried to administer to her. They took her away, screaming.

I paused for a moment, tears welling in my eyes. I glanced at my mother's gown and wedding ring in my hands. The officer continued making notes of my statement.

"And that's when you told the nurse that your mother fell," the officer said.

Distracted, I looked at him. I quickly wiped the tears from my eyes. "Sorry. Yes. I told her she fell walking to a neighbor's house."

"But you weren't there when she fell."

"That's correct."

"Where was your father this entire time?" the officer asked.

"I told you. He was at work."

"Would you be willing to vouch for that?"

"Yes, of course."

The officer glanced through his notes before putting them away. "Your father will have to fill out a detailed timeline of where he has been today and provide the necessary witnesses to corroborate his story," he said. "But I'm sure everything will be all right."

"Is my father going to be arrested?" I asked.

"No." The officer smiled. "We just have to check things out. Your father will be fine. I'm sorry to have to take your time like this. It's just procedure. Thank you for answering our questions. You can see your mother now. The nurse will show you to her."

I thanked the officers and followed the nurse back to the ER. From a distance I could hear Mom screaming. A curtain, half closed, shielded my mother from the rest of the ER. My father was already at the side of her bed, helping the doctors to restrain her. They were forcing liquid charcoal into her mouth. "We found high levels of narcotics in her blood," the nurse said. "The charcoal is just a precaution."

"My mother takes pain medication for her neck," I said. For some reason I felt the need to explain my mother's actions as if there *was* a way to explain them. *She was sexually abused since she was three years old, which has driven her insane. She has several alters living inside her and probably takes the pain pills to deal with her crappy life.* That was what I wanted to say. That was the truth. But no one wanted to hear that, and so I said that my mother took the pills for her neck whether they expected an explanation or not, like a reflex I had honed from my youth.

I watched Mom continue to fight with the doctors. She was wild and violent, like an animal backed into a corner. It was so different from the quiet, frail woman that was my mother. When she saw me, rage filled her eyes and she struggled against the doctors, pushing herself to the edge of the bed. She knelt with charcoal streaming down the sides of her mouth as she gnashed her teeth at me like a rabid dog pulling against the end of its chain in a desperate attempt to strike out at an intruder. I stumbled back, my heart pounding with fear.

Her face was distorted by the swollen eye and gashed skull, giving her a grotesque look. Her speech was slurred but clear enough to be understood. "You did this to me," she said. Blackened spittle dripped from her mouth onto the floor like hot venom from a viper. "You did this to me, Tiffany. I hate you! Do you hear me? I hate you!"

The words bit into me, spreading their poisonous effect throughout my body. I broke down into crying fits, my breathing erratic and uneven. The room spun, becoming a surreal chamber of nightmarish reality. My mother continued sputtering threats and obscenities. "I hate you, Tiffany. I hate you." It was not clear if she was chanting them or if my own mind was replaying the words over and over.

My father, seeing my pain, stepped between my mother and me as if to shield me from the attacks. "She didn't do this to you, Vickie," he said, "I did." My father turned to me, pushing me away from the bed. "I'm sorry," he said. He then pulled the curtain closed, leaving me alone in the darkened ER.

I continued to take shallow breaths. Each sob constricted my chest until it seemed my heart would be crushed under the force. The screams of my mother resounded through the ER like a chorus of demons scratching at my ears, calling me into an ever-deeper abyss of agony. My legs shook, weak and unsteady, but still I continued to stand with my mother's things in my arms. I hugged her bloodstained gown closer to me, hoping to soak up some small scent of my mother's perfume that would bring back a memory of what she was before this cruel thing had occurred, but all that remained was the stale scent of blood.

From the anguish of my injured heart poured out anger toward my mother and what she had done to me. The words were so clear in my head, *I hate.* Yet I could not say them. Instead I forced them deeper, until they were faint cries in the back of my mind. I would not say it. As long as I didn't say it—it wouldn't be true. I reminded myself that it couldn't be my mother saying those things. My mother loved me. It had to be someone else, another alter. With gritted teeth, I repeated, "It's not my mother, it's not my mother," and whispered prayers to an invisible God.

CHAPTER 7
THOU SHALT NOT HATE

"Do you hate your mother?" the counselor asked. I was thirteen, sitting in a chair across from the counselor of my junior high school. She was a tall, slender woman in her low thirties. Her sandy blonde hair was strung back in a bun with a few strands dangling precariously in front of her face as if to taunt her. She brushed them aside as she stared at me. Her face was angelic with slight curves that slowly descended into a gently angled chin. When she smiled, she committed to it, revealing each of her brilliantly white teeth, perfectly straight. She was an attractive woman and held within her a kind of warmth that made one desirous to open up.

I looked to the floor and began nervously tugging at a loose piece of gauze on my newly bandaged hand. I shrugged slightly, not saying a word while twisting the fabric into a tight winding strand. *Thirty-six*, I thought. I had counted the number of squares on the tiled floor. I had counted again, just like my mother did. I hated anything that made me the same as my mother. *I'm not my mother*, I reassured myself, but I didn't believe it. I looked back at the counselor.

"How did that happen?" she asked, pointing to the bandaged hand. Her voice was soft and soothing.

"I got angry," I said.

"What were you angry about?"

I stopped playing with the bandage, rolled my shoulders back, and let out an exaggerated sigh. *Why were there so many questions?* I hated the questions. I didn't want to be here.

"Were you angry at your mom?"

I looked at the counselor with defiance. "Yes, all right. I was angry with my mom. Okay."

"What were you angry about?" the counselor asked.

Each question wore on me. It seemed never-ending. Every time I answered a question there was another, like a tantalizing goalpost that moved ever more distant with every step and would never be reached. I looked at the clock. *She can't keep me here forever,* I thought.

"I wanted to go to a friend's house," I said.

"And your mother wouldn't let you?"

"No. She said I could, but then she wouldn't let me go."

"Why did she change her mind?"

"She didn't change her mind," I said. "She said she never told me I could go. She's always doing that."

"Doing what?"

"Telling me that I can do something and then pretending she didn't tell me I could. That makes me angry."

"Do you think she is lying to you?"

I looked at the floor again. This time I was figuring out the number of black squares compared to the white squares. I say "I," but the truth was I had nothing to do with it. It was my brain. Probably some wire that had come loose, causing me to do things I didn't want to. Just like my mother.

The counselor leaned forward in her chair. She reached out her hand and put it on my cast. "You haven't gotten anybody to sign it."

"It's only temporary," I said.

"Looks like it hurts."

"It's not that bad."

"How did it happen?"

"I was doing dishes, and I accidentally put my hand through one of the glasses," I said. I rubbed the cast as if to console the pain I was remembering. "I cut the knuckle off the ring finger."

"Ouch, that must have hurt."

"It wasn't that bad."

"I bet there was a lot of blood."

"Yes. They had to take me to the emergency room."

"Did they stitch you up?"

"They had to take some of the skin from the side of my hand first because there wasn't enough skin on the knuckle." I remembered seeing the hand after the doctors were through with the surgery. Stitches protruded from every angle on my hand. The skin was blackened and bruised. I was horrified to think of what it would look like after it healed. My only relief was that it was my right ring finger and not my left. If it were my left, my future husband would have to look at it when he put my wedding ring on. I was already concerned about my weight, and the last thing I needed was a husband running from the altar because of my franken-finger.

"You must have been brave to go through that."

I shrugged.

"I need you to be brave now," she said. She squeezed my arm just below the cast, not a tight grip but a soft hugging hold. She lowered her head until her eyes met mine. "Talking about your feelings is a hard thing to do. Sometimes it can be painful, but it is important that you talk about them. Now I am going to ask some hard questions, and I need you to be brave and tell me exactly what you feel."

I turned away from her gaze. "I can't," I said.

"I don't want you to do something you don't want to, but if you talk about these feelings inside you, it will help," she said.

I did want to talk to the counselor. I wanted to tell her everything. I thought if I did she could make it right. But I couldn't.

My mother had sent me to the counselor because she said I had anger issues and she didn't know what to do with me anymore. Somehow she thought the counselor could fix whatever was wrong with me, but she never went to a counselor to fix what was wrong with her.

She had already sent Lydia to a counselor for depression. According to Mom, Lydia was suicidal and needed help. I never thought of Lydia as the type of person who could take her own life. She was often depressed, that was true, but who could blame her? We both had our reasons for the way we acted. They were our way of acting out against a helpless situation. Neither one of us wanted to lash out at our mother, but we had to deal with our feelings in some way, whether we liked it or not. Lydia's way of dealing with her feelings toward Mom was to completely shut herself off and become depressed. My way of dealing was anger.

Just before I went to the counselor, my mother reiterated our household motto: what happens in this house stays in this house. I was expected to be completely honest with the counselor except for those things that pertained to my mother—those secret things that were divulged on the threat of death, not actual death, but the type of silent death that becomes a barrier between the betrayer and the betrayed. My mother made it clear what would happen if we spoke of her secret. We would come back to find her dead body with a note saying, "You did this."

Maybe it would not play out exactly like that, but her threats of taking her life were never taken lightly. She had already made an attempt on her life after Blain, the oldest of my brothers, was born. Dad told us she was on a trip when we asked where she had gone, but we found out later the real reason for her absence. She had been admitted into psychiatric care after an attempted suicide. The death of my grandmother had sent her into a deep depression from which she never fully recovered, and giving birth to a son, who would one day turn into a man, was too overwhelming. Her admittance into the psychiatric hospital was her first step to being diagnosed with DID. The doctors there had diagnosed her with posttraumatic stress disorder and severe depression.

"Will you answer my question?" the counselor asked.

"I'll try," I said. I would try, but I could not betray my mother.

The counselor sat up in her chair, removing her hand from my arm. She picked up a pen and notepad from her desk to take notes and a box of Kleenex that she handed to me. "If you need to cry," she said, "feel free to use as many as you want."

I took the box and rested it on my bandaged hand.

The counselor adjusted herself in her chair, her narrow bottom slipping from side to side finding that right place to settle. She flipped the dangling hair from her face then balanced the notepad on her knee. The whole maneuver was like watching a circus performer balancing on a unicycle atop a tightrope while juggling bowling pins; the entire time I wondered if she was going to fall.

"Now," she said. She was slightly breathless from the exertion. "Let's see. Where were we? Your mother, that was it." She looked at me again, the stray hairs having found their way back. "Do you hate your mother?" she asked.

"No," I lied. "I mean . . . I don't know." The question made me crawl. If I said I hated my mother, true or not, it would betray not only my mother but also everything I believed in. The counselor's eyes bore down on me wanting a straight answer. "I can't," I said.

"It's okay if you don't think you can answer my question."

"No. It's not that." I hesitated. This was the first time I had ever expressed any emotion, and I found it hard to explain exactly how I felt. I wasn't even sure how I felt. "I can't hate her," I said. Though I did not consider myself a liar, it was the first truly honest thing I had said in my life. It was as if the utterance of it revealed everything else as false, artificial in every respect.

"You can't hate her?"

"No."

"Why can't you hate her?"

"I'm not supposed to hate," I said.

"What do you mean, you're not supposed to hate?"

"It's against my belief to hate." Every religion has its own pilgrimage. For Mormons, the ultimate pilgrimage is the journey to become more like our Savior Jesus Christ. While no one expected you to be perfect, they expected you to try. Jesus didn't hate, so I couldn't hate. At least that is how I saw it.

The counselor smiled. "It's true, we don't want to continue to hate people, but hate is a real emotion. You cannot deny it." She put her notebook aside and leaned in. "Whether we want to admit it or not, we feel hate," she said. "If we deny it, we aren't getting rid of it, we are just pushing it deeper and deeper until there is no room to contain it."

"What happens then?" I asked.

"We explode." She gestured to my bandaged hand. "It was no accident that you put your hand through that glass." She looked at me, her eyes accusing.

"I was angry," I said.

"At your mother," the counselor added. "You won't let yourself hate your mother and so those emotions don't have an outlet. They build up and build up until you blow up. Why are you here?"

"Well I'm not crazy if that's what you mean," I said.

"I never said you were crazy," she said. "Are you afraid people will think you are crazy?"

"No."

"You're not crazy."

"I know I'm not crazy." The truth was if my mother could go crazy, then what would prevent me from going crazy? I was just as helpless from preventing that as I was from escaping the situation that was driving me to it. *I will go crazy,* I thought, *if I don't get out of that house.*

"There's nothing wrong with you, either," the counselor said.

"If there's nothing wrong with me, then why am I here?"

"You just need to learn to deal with your emotions so they don't get out of control. Everyone has to do that. I'm just here to help." The counselor sat back again and pulled her notebook to her. "Now," she said, "why do you hate your mother?"

"I don't *hate* my mother," I exclaimed.

The counselor smiled and then violently flicked the stray hairs out of her face as if she were swatting a set of agitating mosquitoes. She began tapping her foot on the tile. She searched the room looking for where to go next.

"Let's go about this a different way," she said. "What do you like to do?"

"Like to do?"

"You know—in your free time."

Where was she going with this? Cautiously I said, "I like to write."

"You do," the counselor exclaimed.

"Yes. I won an award in the second grade."

"Do you still write?"

"Not as much."

The counselor smiled. She stood up from her chair and walked to her bookshelf. It was a disorganized mess of psychology books with catchy titles, none of which held any answers to what I felt inside, only happy suggestions on how to deal with my feelings as if a ticking time bomb could be defused by simply discussing it. There was no simple green wire to cut in order to defuse the hatred boiling inside me, no simple words that would make it okay. Still, within the confines of that simple bookcase the counselor produced the one thing that would save my life. She retrieved a notebook like her own.

She handed it to me.

"What's this for?" I asked. "Am I going to be interviewing you now?"

The counselor said nothing of my slight. She calmly sat back in her chair and faced me. "I want you to write down how you feel," the counselor said.

"What?"

"You said you like to write," she said. "Then write."

"Yes, but . . ."

"Well, then, what's the problem?"

"I don't know what to write," I said.

"I think an award-winning writer such as yourself can think of something," the counselor said. She pulled the strands of hair out of her face and tied them back. They stayed. She sat triumphantly.

"I don't know how to write my feelings," I said.

"What's there to know? If you're happy, write, 'I'm happy' with a big smiley face on the exclamation mark." The counselor gestured the act of writing with exaggerated arm movements, finishing with a flick of her wrist.

"Yes, but how is this supposed to help so that I'm not angry?" I asked. I was more than a little skeptical.

The counselor got serious. She leaned in. "It will get your feelings out," she said, "so they don't build up in here." She pointed to my heart.

I flipped the notebook over in my hand, examining its exterior as if to weigh the possibility of its being a cure for my anger.

"If you're angry," the counselor said, "write it down. If you hate your mother, write it down."

"Oh, I could never write that," I said.

"If you're worried about people seeing it, then throw it away afterward," she said. "Heck, burn it if you want to."

I thought of pages streamed with lines of writing, reading, "I Hate My Mother" tossed into my father's barbecue, with me pouring lighter fluid over them, striking a match, tossing it in, and watching the inferno ensue, the flickering flame illuminating my devilish grin in the low evening light. I smiled at the thought. The counselor smiled too.

"You can even write them like a story if you want," the counselor added.

"What about poetry?" I asked.

"Especially poetry."

The two of us laughed at the thought of a Doctor Seuss rhyme about hating my mother. "The important thing is that you get those feelings out," she said.

I hugged the counselor and walked out the door with my notebook. "I'll talk to you some more in a couple of weeks to see how things are going," the counselor said as she waved good-bye. She would not see me again. My family moved shortly after that visit, but I still remember her counsel. It was the first time in my life that I felt someone truly cared about my sorrow. For the first time, I was allowed to feel.

At home, Mom sat anxiously awaiting news of my visit to the counselor's office. "What did the counselor say?" she asked.

"Nothing," I said. "She just wanted to know why I was angry. That's all."

"What did you tell her?"

"I told her I didn't know."

"Did she ask about me?"

I hesitated. "No."

"You told her about me, didn't you."

"No, Mom, I didn't. I didn't tell her anything."

"I'm the reason you're angry, is that what you told her?"

"No," I said. "I just told her I didn't know."

"You hate me and that's what you told her."

"Ahh. I can't talk to you when you're like this," I screamed.

I was frustrated and angry that I didn't tell the counselor more. *Why was I so loyal to Mom? She didn't deserve it. I should have told the counselor everything.*

"You'll talk to that counselor, but you won't talk to me," Mom said. She was trying to incite an argument so that she could play the part of the victim.

"You won't listen!"

"Well, maybe you wish you had another mother," she said. She began to cry.

Every part of me wanted to shout out, *Yes! I want another mother.* Instead, it remained a quiet scream in my violently beating heart.

Though I said nothing, Mom took this as an acknowledgment that she was right. "Maybe one day you will have your wish and be rid of me," she said. She went to her room and slammed the door.

I walked to my room, passing her door and resisting the need to check on her. It was always a concern that she might make good on her threats, but at that moment I didn't care. I was angry and felt then that being rid of her would not be so bad, a feeling I would punish myself for later. The counselor was right: I hated my mother. Never was it more apparent. There was no way of denying it. It was an emotion that consumed me like fire that consumes a burning ember, giving more heat to its brilliance.

"Why are you so angry with Mom?" my brother Blain asked. He was always protective of Mom. Perhaps he was the only one among us who truly understood her. In his eyes, she was sick, and once the doctors got her medication right, she would be fine. We were just expected to be patient with her.

"Mom started it," I said. I pushed my way to my room. I didn't want another argument.

"If you weren't so angry, you wouldn't have had to go to the counselor in the first place."

"I'm angry because of . . ." I stopped myself. There was no point in saying it. "I guess I'm just angry," I said instead. I looked toward my mother's room as if to peer into its hidden depths, revealing my mother crying uncontrollably in her victimized state. "I guess no one can really change. We are who we are." I went in my room and slammed the door.

I threw myself onto the bed, the notebook still in my arms. Emotions swirled inside of me like some insoluble mixture that would not settle. I looked at the notebook, flipping through the blank pages. Grabbing a pen from my nightstand, I began writing, slow at first, then faster. The words poured out of me as if the mixture of feelings within me was a liquid steadily being drained out upon the pages. It was an exhilarating feeling I had never experienced before. The need to write more took hold of me until I had filled a good portion of the notebook.

I looked at what I had just created. At first it was frightening, then I saw it for what it was—a beautiful stream of emotions—my emotions. Somehow seeing them on the pages comforted me. As long as they remained there, they would not be inside of me, strangling the life from me. They were now apart from me, a distant thing. I wasn't the angry person that had entered the room. I was different. I could be different. The hope elated me. I didn't have to be a victim like my mother. I could change.

I threw the notebook on the nightstand and smiled. *I'm going to need more notebooks,* I thought. I drifted to sleep unaware of anything outside of the calm I felt within, a peace I had not felt for a long time. A peace I would continue to feel through my writing.

CHAPTER 8
REVELATIONS OF THE PAST

"Christ died that we might live," the speaker said. He was standing at the pulpit at the head of the chapel where I sat with Sean and our two sons, Braxton and Cayden. "His love for us is boundless. He loves us all regardless of our transgressions. If you will turn with me to . . ." A few rustles of paper were heard, but most of the congregation simply sat; others struggled to keep their children quiet, a few snored.

I sat with pen in hand, glaring at the page of my notebook. At the top were the words *My Mother,* then row after row of false starts that had been voraciously crossed through. Since my mother's death, the pen flowed less fluidly. The funeral services were days away, and I could not find the words to say for my mother's eulogy. The prolific Tiffany had found herself speechless.

People would expect something from me. They always did. Family and friends had always spoken of my talent for words and my inspirational speeches. In college, I was often called on to speak. My public speaking teacher felt I was a natural. It was such a casual thing that took little thought, but now I remained uninspired. I continued to stare at the part of the page that was still blank, trying to ignore my other failed attempts that jutted like black thorns springing from the page.

"We must have the spirit of Christ in our hearts," the speaker continued. "Without it, we will never find the true love of Christ, the unconditional love we call charity. President Hinckley said . . ."

"President Hickey," Braxton said loudly.

I smiled at the surrounding members who turned to look. I leaned to my son. "It's President Hin-ck-ley," I said. "Hin—Hinckley."

He beamed back at me and said, "Hickey."

"We'll work on it at home." I patted him on the head. Sean laughed. He always thought it funny when children's mispronunciation of words made them sound like something other than the innocent utterances that they were.

"The attributes of charity are patience, longsuffering . . ." the speaker continued.

I tried to write again. *My mother taught me patience,* I wrote and then quickly crossed it out. That was something you wrote when the person was a beast. After all, Hitler taught a lot of people patience, but that didn't mean he was a good person. I needed something that was truthful and sincere. Unfortunately, truthful and sincere may not be the type of thing that one should say at a person's funeral. I loved my mother, but the memories were not always sweet. There had to be something.

I looked around the church for inspiration. Sean sat next to me, play-fighting with Cayden's action figures. "Those are to keep the kids quiet," I whispered to him.

He looked at me with an astonished look. "What?" he said. His voice carried a hint of injury. "I'm being quiet."

I rolled my eyes.

"The Lord sayeth, 'Be as a little child,'" the speaker said.

Sean nudged me with his elbow and gestured to the speaker. "See."

"You're definitely a child," I said.

He smiled and continued playing.

There was little hope of finding a muse with my husband. I continued to search the room. The bishop sat at the front, behind the speaker, watching the members like a shepherd over his flock. He was a good man. I don't think that they would have a bad man be a bishop, but he was particularly kind. Some men were great in wisdom, others in leadership. Our bishop held both qualities. I felt comfortable with him there.

There was a time I did not feel so comfortable in church. Growing up, my family was not as accepted by some of the members. They were friendly enough, always polite, but beneath their pleasant smiles was the hint of falseness. I'm sure they did not wish us to leave, but they did not welcome us either. We were an aberration in their perfect little world.

There has to be a distinction drawn here. It was not the Church itself that rejected us, it was those within the bounds of that community who did. And it was not everyone who made us feel that way. There were only a few who made us feel unwelcome; the rest did what they could to help, never really knowing the help we truly needed. Those who did make us feel unwelcome mostly did so in subtle ways. There were occasions, however, when they became brazen about their dislike of us, for instance, telling their children not to associate with us. My siblings lost several friends this way. Ultimately, the feelings of the parents would distill to their children, forming into the occasional taunt or tease.

It was not a church thing at all. It was a contempt held in the community where we lived, and it's something any community would exhibit when it comes to mental illness. It just happened that some of those faces that looked at us with stilted smiles in the community were the same that greeted us falsely at church. It bothered me to see them there, sitting in the meetings. I had deep-rooted beliefs in my religion. For me, it was more than a superficial puddle of good words and nice thoughts. It was a religion in the true sense, a revealed truth of the world we fought to cope with. To them, church was nothing more than a glossy gathering to weigh their family against the others in the community.

"I have two sons serving in the Church in Bolivia," they would say, their faces gleaming with pride.

The other members would compliment them on the wonderful way that they had raised their children. They would compliment my parents too. Most of my siblings and I would serve missions for the Church. "It is the proof of a mother's hard work to see such fine children," they would say. It was all so false.

Our accomplishments had nothing to do with how we were raised. We had to work for those things. My mother was incapacitated most of the time, and our father was working. While Mom taught us how we should act, her own actions would be a contradiction. I hated that the most, the hypocrisy.

I glanced down at the notepad. The words *my mother was a hypocrite* were written in large, angry letters. I was shocked to see how easily the emotions ran from my pen. Chiding myself at having written such a harsh thing, I quickly blackened in the words, erasing any evidence of such disloyal thoughts.

"An hypocrite," the speaker said, "with his mouth destroyeth his neighbour: but through knowledge shall the just be delivered."

How could I write of a mother I never truly knew? I couldn't.

I glanced at the pew next to ours. There sat a woman a little older than myself. She sat alone. I knew her only by name, and although I referred to her as sister, customary for our church, I knew very little else about her. I am sure there was gossip about her that fluttered about here and there, but I had made every attempt to avoid any of it. Gossip is the silent whispers of scorn and cruelty that our childhood teasing grows into as we get older. Somehow, I preferred the teasing.

The woman was frail and thin, sickly thin. Her face looked hollow, worn with hardships that were never talked about. She wore a nice dress, nothing fancy, just simple. There was nothing unique about her. She was ordinary and common—soaking into the canvas of life while other strokes took the foreground. It was difficult not to lose her among all the other acquaintances. Yet there was a quality about her that was different, as if everything that made her appear the same was a false front, a mask she paraded around, hoping no one noticed. But they did. She was an outcast, not physically, but inwardly. And those that passed the judgment of differences could smell it like hounds on dead game, only they turned their noses up at it.

No one sat by her. No one spoke to her. She came and went like a specter with little disturbance. She was a younger version of my mother in look and action. My heart yearned to reach out to her, but the distance between us in that small chapel seemed endless.

"We are all his children, every one of us," the speaker said. "We are brothers and sisters in the Lord. 'Ye are no more strangers and foreigners, but fellow citizens with the saints, and of the household of God,' Paul wrote."

I wrestled in my seat, trying to overcome the feelings I held inside. I looked at my children and my husband. We were the perfect family. Everything I had always wanted. I remembered as a child, sitting in church, I looked at the other families—the mothers stroking the hair of their daughters. They looked happy. There was no hatred there, no animosity, only love. I felt anger then, too. I was angry that I could not have that. I wished for that normality, that simple perfection that my life lacked.

Love is a simple thing, yet so many of us live without it. We search for it, and never find it. I looked for it in my husband and found it in him, but it is a far different thing to find love in another. I had to find it in myself. Sean proposed three times before I found it in myself. It was there all along; I just did not recognize it. Perhaps I just needed someone to show me that what I felt was love.

"It is said love is a verb, not a noun," the speaker said. "I'm not sure who said it. Elder Something or Other." The congregation laughed in a solemn yet abundant roar. "The point is, we cannot expect God to give us love. We must be willing to act, and then we will find love."

I had acted in marrying Sean and had found love far beyond any I could imagine. Like an endless stream of water from some cosmic faucet, we simply have to turn it on, and it will never end. As a child, I waited for others to turn on that faucet, but no one could. No one can. It is something we must do ourselves. Sean did not make me love him; he showed me how to love by loving me first.

I glanced at the woman sitting across from me and thought of my mother. Like all children, I had been selfish. I wanted love, and in the only way she knew how, Mom had given it to me, but I would not accept it. I wanted a different love, a love I deemed normal, one that would not hurt me later. Somewhere along the way, I stopped loving my mother in order to live with her. Now she was dead, and I didn't know if she ever knew that I loved her. I wasn't sure if she knew anyone loved her.

The people who should have loved her most when she was a child betrayed her. Her father treated her like some kind of filthy object for his devilish delight while her mother allowed it to happen. Yet my mother remained loyal to them. With her husband and children, my mother saw herself as a burden and not as a person who could be loved. Yet she loved us. She was riddled with faults, damaged by a lifetime of pain, and we saw her there, flawed and broken, like a leper on the side of the street, ostracized and untouchable to those around her. Did I go to her? Did I try to help her? I don't know.

I sat with my children and husband, surrounded by the love and praise of friends and family, and there she sat alone, a thing to revile. Why had I not done more? I glanced down at the notepad. It read *I am a hypocrite.* I didn't cross it out. I felt dirty inside—like I was as guilty as my grandfather was. I had betrayed my mother, not in action but in my every inaction. I should have done more.

"I know God's love for us is great, and through his son, Jesus Christ, He has given us a way out of our sins and back to Him," the speaker said. "I know one day we will be united as eternal families, glorified in the Resurrection."

The speaker closed in the name of Jesus Christ, as was customary, then sat down. The bishop said a few remarks and closed the meeting with a hymn and a prayer. I stood up, determined to speak to the woman sitting near us as if that simple act could atone for the countless words I had not spoken to my mother, but as I approached her, members surrounded me like flocking birds.

"I heard about your mother," one said. "I am so sorry to hear about your loss," another said. They offered to bring dinners in for my family and other such services to show their deep concern. They were trying to show their love the only way they knew how. They were trying to mourn with me, but how could they? How could they know what I was going through? I never told them; I held it close, a hidden secret like my mother had kept. Perhaps if I had told them, perhaps if my mother had told them, they really could have helped, or at least understood. The silence was the endless chasm that had divided them from my mother. The same silence that had formed a wall between my mother and me. Our love stretched across that wall like a vine, touching on occasion the other side, but never penetrating it. It is the same wall that divides every community, keeping us from one another like prisoners of social consequence.

I struggled to get to the woman, weaving through people who stood as stationary boulders in my path. My son dragged behind me, like a chain pulling me back. The woman was at the door. I reached out my hand to her but was stopped by another group of members speaking their condolences. I stood watching her open the door, my son tugging at my dress.

I looked at him. He was showing me a drawing he had made of us holding hands in the sun; they are always in the sun at that age. I looked back at the woman who was now walking out the door. A room full of faceless acquaintances stood between us. She glanced back momentarily before leaving. Her face was skewed by the blinding brilliance of the sun reflected in the glass door, transforming it briefly and in its obscurity revealing the face of my mother. I wanted to cry out, to have her come back, but what good would it do? She was gone now and my chances to redeem those years of silence with her.

I began to cry.

Cayden tugged on my dress again. "Why are you crying, Mommy?" he asked.

I knelt down and cupped his cheeks with my hands. I smiled. "Mommy's just sad that Grandma is gone," I said.

"It's okay, Mommy," he said. "My teacher says she'll come back when she's res-resur-rict . . ."

"Resurrected," I said.

He nodded. "Mommy, what does res . . . that thing you said mean?"

"It means we'll see her again."

CHAPTER 9
THE INTRUSION

Cymbals crashed and drums beat in low precautionary tones that rumbled through the stadium. It was the big band competition of my junior year, and nerves were high. This was the big one. Those who won here would be known as the best. My high school had one of the largest bands in the state, and we were top ranked. I played piccolo in the marching band, and while most would gladly have their parents supporting them in this crucial moment of adolescence, having mine here only added to the tension.

It was always precarious having my parents attend school functions, and usually they didn't. When it came to band, however, they saw an opportunity to make up for all the other areas they had neglected. They helped out with band fundraisers by joining the band boosters, lending their time mostly, as money was scarce. While their efforts were appreciated, to the teenage mind it seemed an intrusion. Band was my place of escape. My friends were in band. My greatest memories were in band. It remained a sanctuary of peace from the stresses of home—a happy place where the past could be forgotten and I could enjoy myself. Having my parents there only brought back what I was trying so hard to forget.

"Come on, Mom," I said. "I have to get to the field."

My mother talked flirtatiously to a group of seniors from another school. This was the alter Becky, though at the time it was just another reason to hate my mother. When Becky came out, she acted like a teenager. It wasn't an attempt to reclaim youth or to connect with her teenage daughters, like some parents do. In my mother's mind she was seventeen, a carefree teenager looking for kicks. It is difficult to explain the difference between moods that are normal to everyone and the alters that my mother had. These were not whimsical fascinations that undertook her at times, like the donning of a new dress. They were abrupt and distinct. She was someone else; it was the same dress but worn by a different person.

Growing up, I knew this behavior was not normal, but I had no way of explaining it. I only knew that I saw my mother acting out different parts like an actor on a stage. To me they were intentional. When she denied having acted a certain way, it was more deception. It never occurred to me that she might be telling the truth, that she really did not know what the other alters were doing. In my eyes, my mother, the same person who taught us as young children never to lie or God would know, was riddled with lies and deceit.

I grabbed my mother's arm and dragged her away from the boys. She waved to them playfully. "What's eating you?" she asked. "I'm just talking."

"You're a married woman," I said. "That's what's wrong."

My mother looked at me but said nothing.

Why did she have to act like that? I thought. *Why couldn't she just be normal?*

"Tiffany," a voice called from the crowd. It was my friend Kalli.

She ran toward me with piccolo in hand. Without stopping, she embraced me like a tidal wave crashing against the shore. She was much taller than me, with medium-length hair that she kept in ringlets that bounced whenever she moved. "Martha is here too," she said.

"Where?" I asked.

"Over there." She pointed into the crowd at a petite girl with short hair carrying a trumpet. Seeing us, Martha waved enthusiastically, nearly dropping her trumpet.

Kalli turned to me, grabbing my shoulders and hopping up and down. "Isn't it so exciting?" she said. "So many cute guys to choose from!" She laughed then, seeing my mother, quickly quieted. "Oh, hi, Mrs. Young."

Mom smiled brightly. "Hi, Kalli." Her voice was not that of a parent but a school-aged girl. "I'm excited too. I can't wait to see you guys perform." She hopped up and down, mimicking my friend's behavior.

It was fun to hang out with my mother when Becky came out. It was like having another sister rather than a mother, but that was also the problem. Too often I needed a mother, and she wasn't there. Friends and sisters I had plenty of, but a mother I had none. Seeing Mom behave like an adolescent in front of my friend embarrassed me. I wanted to get away, but I felt responsible for looking after her until Dad returned.

I looked back to the entrance of the stadium to see if I could spot him. Lydia was at home taking care of the younger children so Mom and Dad could devote their full attention to the needs of the band. And although my parents had no children to care for, we were still late as usual, and my father had decided to drop us off at the entrance while he parked the car. There was no telling how long he would be. By the number of people there, the only parking places available would be a long walk from the stadium.

"How long will it be before we perform?" I asked.

"I don't know, but Mr. Wayman wants us to line up anyway," Kalli said.

I searched the entrance again for a sign of my father's balding head. Turning to my mother, I said, "Mom, I have to go line up."

"Go right ahead," Mom said. She was swaying to the band music playing in the distance. "I'll be watching."

"Mom, you need to stay here until Dad comes."

"Yes, Honey," she said. She seemed distracted.

"Promise me you will stay here for Dad," I said.

"I will," she said. "Now go have fun with your friends."

I walked away with a nervous feeling. "Come on, let's go talk to Martha," Kalli said. She grabbed me by the arm and began running across the field. I looked at my mother as she stood swaying until she became lost in the confusion of the crowd.

The band stood in straight, rehearsed rows, each member with instrument in hand. Mr. Wayman stood at the front, giving his last words before the performance.

"Okay, everyone," he said. He gestured for everyone to quiet down. "Now, we have been practicing all year for this. You guys are the best I've had, the best in the state. Let's show it to the judges."

The band cheered.

"Remember to follow that person in front of you. No matter what, don't take your eyes off their backside."

Laughter erupted.

"You know what I mean," he said. He looked at the judges. Another band was in the middle of their performance. "We go when the signal is given. Okay?"

Everyone nodded. We looked at each other and sighed, trying to rid ourselves of the last strands of tension. A few tested their instruments to ensure they were tuned properly. This was it, the starting gates. Now we waited restlessly for the starter's gun.

"Tiffany!" Kalli cried. She was weaving between the ranks.

"What are you doing?" I asked. "We're going to be performing soon."

"I had to tell you." She leaned over, attempting to catch her breath. "It's your mother," she said.

"What about my mother?"

"She's been in some sort of accident on the field."

"What happened? Is she hurt?"

Kalli shook her head. "I don't know."

"All right, get ready," Mr. Wayman said. "We're on."

Kalli looked at me with grief in her eyes and mouthed the words, "I'm sorry." She ran back to her position in the line.

The band began to move, but I stood motionless, my mind reeling from the news. I had to get to my mother. An instrument butted me in the back. "Get going," said the voice behind it.

I marched out with the rest of the band onto the field. I watched the person in front of me distractedly. The focus I had worked so hard to obtain before the performance was now gone. The band turned, then I turned. I was lapsed in time, like an awkward thorn protruding from a bouquet of flowers. How could the judges not see?

I strained to remember the footwork, but every thought led me to my mother. I listened to the beat of the percussion, searching for my place in the music. I played, but it was too late. I was off. The notes came out dull and exasperated. There was nothing behind them. I had lost all effort.

My steps fell heavy as I continued the performance halfheartedly. All my thoughts were on Mom. The only thing I was sure of was that she had been in a serious accident, but were those the exaggerated details of a secondhand messenger or the cushioned news of a friend? I fought to keep up with the rest of the band, which seemed to be treading over me. I wanted the world to stop; yet it continued without me.

An ambulance siren sounded in the distance, faint at first but increasing until it was an obtrusive note in our performance. Streams of alternating red-and-white light descended on the stadium bleachers. Although I could not see the commotion generated by the spectacle, I remained aware. Our entire performance seemed affected by it, and yet we continued to march, trying to ignore the disturbance. It was a battle for attention. Despite those things that deter us from our path, we must march on or be lost in the flood of everyday affairs.

The performance ended as disheveled as it had begun. There was an air of relief that the ordeal was finished, which settled into disappointment as each mistake was replayed in my mind. It was the same process that I have felt at countless performances, but this time I felt the mistakes were all mine. If we lost, it would be because I was not focused. I pushed the guilt aside like an unfinished task that I would complete later. More immediate emotions took the foreground.

I raced to my mother, ignoring the calls from friends and acquaintances. I pushed through the crowd of onlookers who had gathered around the ambulance. On the other side, Mom lay on the bed of a trailer, her leg twisted awkwardly. Dad stood above her, directing the paramedics. They lifted her onto the gurney, despite her insistences that she was fine. Seeing her struggle with the paramedics brought some relief and some embarrassment. *Why did she always have to fight?*

"What happened?" I asked my father.

"She became disoriented and wandered onto the track," Dad said. She got hit by a band trailer."

"I'm so sorry, I didn't see her," the driver of the trailer said. "She just walked right into me."

I watched as the paramedics lifted her into the ambulance. "Well, is she going to be okay?" I asked.

"She's probably broken her leg, but other than that, she seems all right," Dad said. He jumped down from the trailer and hugged me. "Don't worry. She'll be fine."

I shook my head and wiped tears from my eyes.

The paramedics closed the doors to the ambulance. My mother could still be seen through the window. The siren sounded again, and the ambulance pulled away, leaving my father and me standing alone in a circle of spectators. My friends gathered, expressing their concern.

I was relieved then angry. The most important event in my young life, and it had been ruined. If she weren't the way she was, this wouldn't have happened. She was a constant source of embarrassment and shame. *Why did she have to be here?* I thought. *Why couldn't she just stay home?*

I imagined the other members of the band hating me for bringing her and ruining the performance. I had let them down, not intentionally but because I had a mother who was different. She was a burden to me, a loathsome albatross that I would never be rid of. I looked into the faces of my friends. They only cared about me, but I didn't want them there. I didn't want them to see my mother. If they knew what she was like, what my home life was like, they would not want to be near me. I was an oddity, like my mother. Only, I didn't choose this, and in my mind, she had.

"Let's go," I said to my father.

"You can stay with your friends and ride down with them," he said.

"Yeah. My mom can take you home," Kalli said.

"No. I want to see Mom," I said. It was a lie. The last person I wanted to see was my mother, but I didn't want to remain there either. I had to leave. I had to escape.

Together my father and I walked to the car. Neither of us spoke; we were both tired.

CHAPTER 10
ESCAPE

"Are we there yet?" Tammy asked. She sighed with that expression of boredom that accompanies sixteen-year-old teenagers on road trips. I was eighteen and was plenty bored myself. The bus slugged along the interstate on its way to San Francisco.

"We'll be there soon enough," I said. We had embarked on our first trip away from home. It was the summer band trip, and while the purpose was to perform at several different venues, it was the least of our motivations for going. We were going to see San Francisco, the ocean, and most of all we were leaving home. It may have only been for a week, but it was still a relief. It was freedom that we breathed from the rusty vents of the bus.

"We passed the state line hours ago," Tammy said.

"What? You got a hot date or something?" I teased.

"You should be talking. I hear you got a date with one of the trombone players. What's his name? Br-Brenda."

"Britney!"

"I knew it was some sort of girl's name."

"It's not just a girl's name."

"Apparently to some."

"Besides, it's not a date," I said. "All the senior band members are going to see *Phantom of the Opera* together."

"You like him, don't you?" She said it loud enough so the entire bus could hear.

I placed my hand over her mouth and then looked to see if anyone had heard. The entire bus was oblivious to our conversation. I turned to my sister, a scowl stretched across my face. "We're just friends," I said emphatically.

Tammy licked my hand cupped over her mouth.

I quickly withdrew it. "Eww," I said. "You're disgusting."

She ignored the remark. "Friends or not, you're still going together," she said.

Tammy had a comic charm to her that often led her to antagonizing her older siblings. One time while going through a car wash, she put her flippers and diving mask on and began screaming, "I'm drowning. I'm drowning." I can still see her in the backseat making exaggerated gasping motions in the window while other customers watched with concerned looks. Though she was funny and that's what I loved about her, there is nothing more annoying than a younger sister with comedic flare.

"It's not a date, and Britney and I are just friends."

"So does Mom know you're going on a date?" Tammy asked and then quickly added, "I don't think she would approve."

"It's not a date!" I exclaimed. This time the bus did hear.

My sisters and I hardly dated at all. We didn't have much of any social life. Most of our time was spent taking care of Mom and our younger siblings. The only friends we had were from band, and we did not dare bring them to our house. Between the disastrous upkeep of the home and our mother's eccentric moods, the humiliation would be unbearable.

"Oh, come on," Tammy said. "I would love to go on a date."

"I'm sure you will have plenty of guys asking you," I said.

While Lydia and I struggled with weight issues, Tammy remained skinny and petite. Despite her beauty, she remained blind to it, always denying it. My mother was the same way. There was a time when my mother was a young girl during which she deliberately gained weight, thinking that if she was no longer attractive to my grandfather, the abuse would stop. It didn't. Instead his fury against my mother was kindled. He told her she was ugly and that no one would want her, and she was lucky that he wanted her at all. She quickly lost the weight to quench his wrath, adopting the habits of bulimia, which she continued into her adult life.

In a way, my sisters and I carried similar scars to our mother's, as if our grandfather's abuse stretched past our mother to strike us too. My mother often talked of men as being something to fear. She had a natural hatred of all men. Even my father seemed an enemy to my mother. He was one of "them," and she despised him for it. It may not have been intentional, but it was there. We all felt it, even my brothers, who often questioned Mom's feelings toward them. Now that my sisters and I were old enough to date, it was difficult not to see all boys as young predators waiting to ravish our innocence.

"Do you think the family is all right?" Tammy asked.

I had been waiting for the question, straining not to ask it myself. "I'm sure they're fine," I said. "Lydia's there."

Having at least one sister at home brought some relief, but it was difficult to be completely without worry. There was always that subtle discomfort that at any moment our amusement would be interrupted by news of our mother. It was a constant thought that had to be subdued and plunged beneath the depths of consciousness. No matter how deep the thought was forced, though, it would in time bob its head above the surface, and its presence would have to be recognized.

"There it is!" one of the band members exclaimed. "The ocean."

We all leaned out the windows to see.

The ocean emerged beneath the wall of blue sky, creeping its way over the horizon. It was slight at first, like a mirage in the distance, and then it burst into life. Waves pounded one upon another, creating white crests and broken lines. It was violent and calm all at the same time. I imagine that if music could be seen, it would be the same—a beautiful harmony of blue hues infused with erratic, precautionary beats of crashing waves, smooth and steady. I had to think to breathe.

In that moment there was no thought of home. There was only that moment of pure elation. I had found the thing I had been searching for—escape. The only question that remained was how long would this last?

We spent the next few days exploring the novelties of the San Francisco Bay area. We visited Fisherman's Wharf, where the cool air breathed of the sea and the clam chowder warmed our eager stomachs. It was served in hot, steaming sourdough bread bowls. The soup was probably as good as any other I had tasted, but in that place with the ocean crashing below and the salty air surrounding us, it became something else. It was an experience more than a food, vivid and consuming. It was an experience I have not forgotten and could never re-create.

At the hotel, we stayed in rooms together, spending the night painting each other's nails and talking about boys. My pious upbringing would never allow me to talk about men as sexual objects, so instead of rating their backsides, we would rate their shoes as if that was the focus of our attention. We knew differently.

I had very few experiences as a teenager that brought me as much joy as that band trip. It was the close friends and the enticements of a world made fresh. It was seeing new and strange places, experiencing new and strange things. It was the ocean. It was everything that wasn't my home. It was freedom.

Our performance was simply an afterthought.

"So is that the dress you're wearing to the opera?" Tammy asked.

It was a long, black dress with a white, lacy top. I bought it because it looked like something one of Jane Austen's characters would wear. I had an obsession with anything Regency because of the writings of Austen and others like her. I had built a fantasy of what life would have been in those days, going to balls and being courted by young, handsome men. It was a fairy tale I longed for. Having the dress seemed to bring it to life.

I twirled in the bathroom, admiring the dress in the mirror.

"It's beautiful," she said.

"It better be," I said. "I spent an entire paycheck on it." A lot of my money went to help pay bills for my family, but this I had kept for myself. I wanted this occasion to be special.

"So how are you getting there?" Tammy asked.

"We're taking the bus," I said. "What are you going to be doing tonight?"

"I'm going to go to a mystery dinner with the rest of the band."

"Sounds like fun."

"It will be," she said. Tammy lay on the bed spreading her arms over the sheets. "Isn't it wonderful, not having to worry about anything?" She sat up. "I mean, don't get me wrong. I still worry."

"I know what you mean," I said. "It is nice."

"Then why do I feel bad?"

"I feel guilty too."

"I can't help but think that there is something wrong. That something bad is going to happen."

"Nothing bad is going to happen. Lydia is with Mom."

"But she's all alone."

"She can handle it."

"She won't be there much longer."

"What do you mean?" I asked.

"She told me she was thinking of serving a mission for the Church."

"Well, she's almost old enough," I said. I was happy for my sister leaving, but at the same time it meant more responsibility for me. I was bitter, but at least Tammy would be there.

"She's leaving," Tammy said, "and soon you'll be leaving."

"I won't be leaving for a long time."

"I don't want to be alone, taking care of Mom."

"You'll have Blain and the others."

"But without you two . . ." Tammy paused. She tried to choke back the emotion welling up inside of her. "I can't do it. I want to leave too."

I sat down next to her and put my arm around her. "Everything will be all right. I'll be there. Don't worry."

Tammy looked up at me. She gave a slight laugh. "You remember that time you wanted to play school with the kids Mom babysat, but they didn't want to play?"

"Yes," I said. "You and Mom both won't let me forget."

"You sat them all in front of the chalkboard and tied them to the chairs so they couldn't leave. When Mom saw what you did, she was so mad."

"Yes. She really laid into me then."

"And when Dad came home."

We both laughed.

"I used to be so afraid of you after that," Tammy said, "but now I wish I could somehow keep you and Lydia from leaving."

"Well, I don't think tying us to chairs will work."

We laughed even more.

"Tammy," I said. "I won't leave you alone."

Tammy pushed me away. "Go on," she said. "Get your dress on and get out of here, or you'll miss your date."

"It's not a date," I said.

"Can't be much of a date if you're going on a bus."

That evening I sat in the balcony overlooking the stage. It was the first time I had been to any stage performance that wasn't put on by our church group and put together in less than an hour. The stage setting was enormous and the special effects breathtaking. I became enthralled in the artistry of the story, of a young girl trying to escape the dark forces that seduce her to stay. Her emotions were so real. It was as if I were that girl.

She desperately wanted to run away with her young love, but something kept her from leaving. Perhaps it was the fear of the Phantom and what he might do that kept her from leaving. Perhaps it was a feeling of obligation to him for what he had given her. Despite her hatred of the Phantom, she knew that he loved her. The Phantom could not bear to see her leave, and so he struck out against her and those who tried to take her away from him.

I cried for her, thinking there would be no escape until the Phantom was dead. Though she finally ran away with her love, I don't think she ever escaped that phantom of her past. It would always be with her, haunting her.

The trip passed rapidly and soon we were back at the school. Tammy and I waited several hours for our parents, but they never came. They had forgotten. Finally, our band instructor found us a phone to call my father. He picked us up on the way home from his second job.

When we got in the truck, Dad said nothing about being late, not that I had expected it. "Where's Mom?" I asked.

"I don't know," he said. He seemed upset. "She's probably at home."

"How was work?" I asked.

He said nothing; his thoughts were elsewhere.

"Is everything all right?"

He looked at me hesitantly, as if he were avoiding something. He glanced at my instrument case. "How was your trip?" he asked.

"Fine," I said. "What's wrong?"

He turned to face the road. There was a long pause. With a few false attempts, he said, "I lost my job at the pallet yard."

"What? But how?"

"Things were slow, so they laid me off. Said he didn't need a mechanic."

"What are you going to do?" I asked. A nervous feeling of uncertainty swept over me. I had seen my parents struggle through enough financial troubles that I knew what losing a job meant.

"A friend of mine knows a guy who needs a mechanic," he said. "It doesn't pay as much, but I can probably make up the difference with hours."

It was hard enough having Dad gone so much. Now he may have to be gone even longer. *I shouldn't have gone on the trip*, I thought. *I shouldn't have spent all that money on a dress. I should have saved it for my family.*

My father put a hand on my shoulder and smiled. "Don't worry," he said. "It will work out."

We pulled up to the house; it was the same as I had left it. While this brought some relief, it was a bitter relief.

"I have to go back to the palette yard," Dad said. "I have to pick up my tools."

"Can I come?" Tammy asked.

"All right," he said. "You want to come, Tiffany?"

"No," I said. "I'll stay here with Mom."

I stepped out of the car and walked to the door, pausing slightly to wave good-bye. Inside, Mom sat in the recliner, a half-eaten plate of food on her lap. Chewed-up pieces of food ran down the front of her blouse as her mouth gaped open. She had passed out while eating.

I took the plate off her lap and with my fingers scooped the food from her mouth so she wouldn't choke. I then cleaned what I could off her clothes and helped her into bed. She said nothing the entire time, slipping in and out of consciousness but never registering that I was even home. After pulling the covers over her and kissing her on the cheek, I went to my room and wrote. It was all I could do. I had never truly escaped.

CHAPTER 11
FINDING MOM

Mom died on the night my parents celebrated their thirty-first anniversary. It was not an intimate evening, my parents had few of those, but it was a nice evening, spent as longtime companions. The evening was spent at a restaurant and then at home, watching an old movie, the old black-and-white kind, possibly Doris Day in her younger years. My father of course dozed off during the movie, snoring as he did. My mother didn't mind. She was fine just being in his arms. Then, at the end of it all, my father went to bed—he had work the next morning—and my mother stayed up. From then until her death it is impossible to know what occurred.

My brother Chris came home from a date around two in the morning, waking my father. Dad got up from bed and noticed my mother kneeling at the edge. My father was angry at seeing my mother passed out again because she had taken too much medication. He began yelling at her to get back in bed, but there was no response. He then grabbed her arm and noticed it was limp and cold. Pulling her face into the light, he saw it was rigid and blue. He screamed for help.

"Chris, help me!" he said. "She's dead, Christopher, your mother's dead! I don't know what to do."

Chris quickly came to the room. He called 911 and was instructed to do CPR. He peeled back the edges of her mouth;

rigor mortis had already made them stiff. He breathed into her mouth and then began compressions on her chest. With each compression, he could feel her ribs buckle with dull cracking sounds. Though he knew she was dead, he continued to pump on her chest while Dad sat in the corner pleading for him to save her.

"Don't leave me here," Dad said. "Don't leave me alone."

Tammy and her husband, Jeremy, who lived with my parents at the time, hurried their children into a bedroom upstairs. "They can save her," she said. "They save people with CPR, right? She's going to be okay."

The look on Jeremy's face was not reassuring.

When the paramedics arrived, they did little. She had been dead awhile. Any attempt to save her had been in vain. They placed her on a gurney and covered her with a sheet. The police arrived too. They searched the house for any prescription medication that could have been the cause of her death. After taking reports, they left with the paramedics, leaving the family to mourn.

Having heard the details of Mom's death from each of my siblings who had been witnesses, I still didn't find it any more real when I stepped into that bedroom after my mother's death. I stared at the place where Mom's body had been resting, imagining her lying there prostrate in the act of prayer. What was she praying for? Did she pray for God to spare her life or receive it willingly? I shuddered at the thought of it.

I sat down next to my sisters, who had pulled photographs from the closet and began sifting through them for pictures of Mom that would be placed in the memorial slide show at her viewing. My brothers joined us as well, looking over our shoulders and commenting as we dug through the piles.

"Look at this," Tammy said. She was pointing at a permission slip signed by Mom. It had the name Vicky crossed out, then the name Vickie written next to it at the bottom. "Remember how we had to remind Mom that her name ended with an 'ie'?"

"That was Vicky," I said.

"I had her change the name on the permission slip," Tammy said. "I thought the teacher might think I tried to forge it if it was spelled wrong. But it looks like the teacher never even received it."

Vicky spelled her name differently than Mom. When we confronted her about it, she would quickly change it as if forgetting to spell her own name were a momentary lapse of memory. Mom's alters hated being confronted with something pertaining to the other alters, as if it called their own existence into question, making them realize that they were nothing more than a figment of my mother's psyche.

Dissociative identity disorder is difficult for people to accept because it makes us question one of the fundamental aspects of reality: our own identity. Who we are is based so much on our memories and experiences, both of which are out of our control. If our memories are horrific and our experiences depraved, we seem doomed to be the same, nothing more than a product of destiny. It is reassuring to think that we can choose how we will react to life, and that is how we identify ourselves. But what happens when the very identity that determines how we react can change? What if our own mind could be tampered with by means that lie outside of our control?

Our entire court system is based on the fact that a criminal is responsible for his choices and should rightly be punished for them, even if that punishment means death. We accept this view because victims need their retribution as if the punishment of another could rectify the pains of the afflicted. My own religion is based on an undeniable principle of agency. We believe that God's great design is that each man and woman should choose good from evil. The idea that a person could be so conflicted in their actions makes it difficult to conform to such belief systems.

The acceptance that we have no control over who we are leads to even more grave dilemmas. How do we identify ourselves if we are nothing more than the random constructions of experience? How can we change? How can we be held accountable for what we do? We have no more control over our destiny than a drop of water swept away indistinguishable in the ocean's current. Are we nothing more than creatures of fate? Is agency just an illusion?

My mother's very existence represented all those contradictions. She was hated not just for what she did, but also for the intrusion on that reality to which we so eagerly cling. To accept her is to accept those contradictions and the knowledge that they may never be resolved. Like a Pandora's box waiting to be opened, she walked through the lives of so many. Some chose to ignore her, never discovering her true contents and thereby sustaining their perfect image of the world. Others reached out to her and were burned by the very idea of her. For my family, we had no choice but to accept her. She was our mother, and we loved her as much as we could understand her.

"I loved Vicky," I said. "She was the nice one. She always made soup for us and stroked our hair when we were sick."

"No, that was Julie," Tammy said. "Julie was the caretaker, Vicky was our protector."

"Didn't Dad have a protector?" I asked. "What was her name?"

"Julia," Lydia said.

"How do you know their names?" Blain asked.

"Veronica told us," Tammy said.

Lydia and Tammy spent much of their high school years at home, caring for Mom. When Lydia became sick, Tammy stayed home to help out. After Mom was diagnosed with DID, Tammy became curious. While she was home with Mom, Tammy decided to question her about the alters. Mom always denied she had them, but other alters, like Veronica, were more open about them. The doctors had only identified a handful of distinct alters, but with the help of Veronica, who came out on occasion, we were able to identify more and even acquired descriptions of some of them.

In addition to herself, Mom had fourteen alters. Three of those alters were children: Sam (a boy), Tina, and Vicki. I hated Vicki because she was always whining and negative. Sam was timid and rarely spoke, and Tina yearned for knowledge and was a perfect speller. There were the protectors: Julia for Dad, Vicky for us, and John for Mom. The protectors' job was to protect family members from being harmed, especially by Bill, the violent alter.

In addition to these alters, there was Victoria, the drill sergeant who always expected perfection; Linda, who had an incessant need to bake (possibly created to fill the gap that Grandma left at her death); Julie, who was always showing kindness, caring for others' needs before her own; and Vivica, who took care of business matters and had the desire to one day own a business of her own.

Other alters came out to cope with different events in Mom's life. Sandy was the promiscuous woman who came out during my parents' intimacy. Although she was only eighteen, she knew a great deal about anything of a sexual nature. Becky was the other teenager, always bubbly and flirtatious. Finally, there was Veronica, who knew everything about the others but never completely admitted that she was a part of them.

Each alter had its own uniqueness, like rooms within the same house. Each room had its role and function, and each brought memories of our mother. It was difficult to separate Mom from all the alters. They all existed together within the same house with only one out at a time. When an alter came out, Mom would step aside. To her these little episodes were blackout spells. She had no memory of them and did not wish to acknowledge them. She had spent her entire life being subdued by men with no control of her body. When she thought she had finally escaped, it would be her own mind that would subdue her, taking advantage of her body and making her do things she did not want to do.

We looked at the photographs that spanned our lifetimes. Some had just been developed after years of being in a film canister while others were worn and dilapidated. Each told the story of a scene that once existed, proof that our lives were there—we did exist and Mom with us. There were pictures of birthdays and of Christmas. Though my father's income was meager, they tried to provide some recognition of these events, giving what gifts they could manage. I picked up a picture of my mother in a swimsuit standing by a small children's wading pool. She had a large straw sun hat and large brown sunglasses. She was smiling.

"She was beautiful," I said. "She was always beautiful, even if she wouldn't admit it."

"She was always down on her looks," Tammy said.

"Not always," Lydia said.

"Remember when she would get in those moods?" Lydia said. "She would walk around the house, showing off her lingerie."

"Oh and those Harlequin romance novels she always read," I added.

My mother was a pious, upstanding woman who taught us the ways of the Church: no sex before marriage. She even made anything to do with sex seem dirty and depraved. However, there were occasions when Sandy came out. Sandy was a less conservative woman. She saw sex as a wonderful thing and our bodies as beautiful temples to be respected. It was Sandy who gave us our first instructions in sex, much to our horror.

"Mom you don't have to explain this to us," I said. "We already learned about it at school."

"Yes, but they don't tell you everything," my mother said.

Lydia sat silent. It was difficult to tell whether she was being complacent or was petrified at the thought of having my mother talk to us about sex. We had never even seen an R-rated movie, let alone discussed the details of the sexual act. In the Mormon faith, sex is sacred and reserved for married couples only. That was the vow I had made since a young child in Sunday School. I had made it a point not to think about it until I was actually going to get married.

"Now, I have gone to the library and checked out a few books on the subject," Mom said. She sat several large volumes on the table in front of us. "I want you to go through these and ask any questions you may have."

"But Mom . . ."

"No buts," she said. "I want to make sure you are prepared."

Lydia opened one of the books to a page with a nude man. Her face flushed red, and her eyes became big. She quickly closed the book.

"This is so embarrassing," I said.

"There is nothing to be embarrassed about," my mother said. "Your body is a beautiful thing."

I pinched the fat around my waist. "This is beautiful?"

"Of course it is. You should be proud of your bodies. Now, I take it you know where babies come from."

"Mom!" I exclaimed.

Mom looked at the page and then back at us. "What?" she asked. It was as if such a thing was commonplace. "You're going to have to see it some time. Better now."

Lydia covered her eyes in shame.

I got up from the table. "That's it," I said. "I will never get married."

I did get married, and in preparing for that night it was the alter Sandy who helped me pick out my lingerie. Despite my reservations due to my weight, she made me feel that I could be confident. She always made me feel better about my body.

My brothers and Tammy laughed as they thought of my mother explaining sex. It was such a contrast from how she usually acted.

"I can't believe Mom would do that," Chris said.

"Mom did lots of crazy things," I said.

"I know that, but . . ."

"You had it easy," I said. "Mom used to bounce quarters off our beds to make sure we made them correctly." This was actually Victoria in her drive for perfection.

"No way," Heidi said. She was the youngest of us and had never known the mother that existed before Grandma died, before Mom gave up. After she gave up, Victoria only came out occasionally when the house needed cleaning for a guest or when we needed scolding for our less-than-perfect grades. I imagine it was difficult for Victoria to live in such imperfect conditions.

"Look at this," Lydia exclaimed. She showed us a picture of a wedding cake.

"What about it?" Chris asked.

"You know how Mom used to be a cake decorator?" Lydia said. "This must have been one that she made."

"Mom always liked baking with Grandma," I said. "Remember when she would just suddenly get the urge to bake?"

"Linda," Tammy said. "She was the one who always cooked."

"I remember when she almost fell out of the camper on vacation," Blain said. "If Chris and I hadn't caught her, she would have completely fallen out."

It was the last vacation that we went on as a family. My father had borrowed a camper from a friend at work and decided to take a driving tour up the West Coast to Oregon. Along the way, while driving down the interstate, Mom got the sudden urge to make some sandwiches for the family. Dad demanded she sit back down, and we told her we weren't hungry, but she insisted. While we were trying to get her to sit down, Dad had to swerve, and out she went. She slammed against the back door of the camper, forcing it open. My brothers, who were by her at the time, grabbed on to her arms while she dangled in traffic.

"That was the worst family vacation ever," I said. "After that, I promised myself I would never go on another vacation with Mom."

We laughed about the incident and many others. It was a testament of resilience to be able to laugh at those things that brought so much pain. Like the photographs, our memory was a collection of joyous memories tattered and torn by the reality of what we had lived through, a mother with DID. We laughed and smiled outwardly, but these were shallow emotions, like a thin film covering what lay deeper.

"There's not very many photographs here," Tammy said.

"Mom and Dad didn't take many photographs," Lydia said.

The photographs seemed to dwindle in the recent years as if the desire to remember had faded. Heidi rummaged through each photograph. There were few pictures of her as a child.

"Here's one of you, Chris," I said. I handed him a picture of Mom carrying a baby into the house. My sisters huddled around, admiring. "Cute little 'Kissifur.'" *Kissifur* was a cartoon when we were children. It was about a little bear named Kissifur. We always teased Chris with the nickname.

"I hated that nickname," he said.

"We know," Lydia said. She laughed.

"And that other one," Chris said.

"Christopher-Crash," I said.

"Yes, that one."

"Why did you call him Christopher-Crash?" Heidi asked.

Tammy, Lydia, and I looked at each other, smiling. "You don't know the story," I said. "When Chris came home from the hospital, they got in a car wreck.

* * *

"Are you ready yet, Vickie?" Dad asked. They were in the hospital room. "We need to get home." He was carrying several bags and had flowers tucked under his arm.

"I just want to put my clothes on before we go," Mom said.

"Just leave your bathrobe on," Dad said. He grunted, trying to grip the bags tighter.

"I don't want people to see me in my bathrobe."

Dad had no patience for this type of female reasoning. He was quite content with walking out the door with a broken zipper on his pants and a grease stain across his face. "We're going straight home," he said. "No one is going to see you in your robe who hasn't already."

"I don't know, George," Mom said. She was hesitant.

"It'll be fine, Honey," he said. "The kids are waiting to see you."

It was true we were all waiting to see Mom. As neglectful as she may have been at times as a mother, Dad was worse. Mom had instructed my father before she went to the hospital to make sure we had a hot meal and took our daily vitamin. The hot meal consisted of toasted peanut butter and jelly sandwiches, and he mixed up the daily vitamin with a bottle of rosemary, which he insisted we take despite our complaints that it tasted funny.

After more coaxing, Dad managed to get Mom into the car wearing only her robe. The nurses placed Christopher in my mother's arms. In those days, no one thought of driving safety. They left the hospital with Mom holding Christopher and got to the first stoplight before a car failed to stop and slammed into the passenger side of the car. The driver ran to my parents' car to assess the damage. Seeing Mom holding the baby, he exclaimed, "Oh no, she's got a baby," and ran back to his car and drove off.

The police arrived then the paramedics then the camera crew. A woman getting into a hit-and-run accident after just leaving the hospital with her child was big news in a small town, and my mother would be seen on every television for miles around, walking around in her bathrobe. She never let my father forget his making her leave the hospital in nothing more than a bathrobe, and we never let my brother forget, nicknaming him Christopher-Crash.

While the memory was amusing, the car crash marked a decline in my mother's behavior that spiraled out of control, culminating in her death. My mother's nagging neck pain turned into a ruptured disk. She was prescribed pain medication, which led to her dependency. Despite my mother's objection to taking medication, she developed a severe drug problem. It was uncertain whether she did it knowingly or under the cloak of lapsed memory. However, it was certain that her episodes became more frequent and her violence more pronounced. She soon lost any control she had once had.

"Here's a photo of you, Tammy," Blain said. He handed her a photograph.

"This isn't me," she said. "This is Tiffany." She passed the photo to me.

I looked at it. It was a picture of my mother holding me as a baby. She was young, much younger than I had ever known her. She was smiling up at the camera, cradling me in her arms. I had not seen that expression on her face. It was not the expression of one of the alters. It was not the expression of years of wear. It was the expression of joy—the expression of love.

Tears welled in my eyes. It was difficult to say that my mother was ever happy. She always seemed to have that solemn distance of all victims of trauma, but in that picture she was smiling, not the false smile she often used—this was real. In that moment, captured by film, was an instant where my mother was happy, and I was the cause. In that one picture I had found the mother I longed for.

I wiped the tears from my eyes.

"Do you think . . ." I hesitated. "Do you think it was suicide?" I asked.

My family looked at the photographs, none wanting to face me, no one wanting to say.

"No!" a voice said. It was my father, standing in the doorway. "I don't want to hear anyone say that it was."

"But what about Bill?" I asked.

"Bill was gone," he said. His voice carried a determined finality. He had made up his mind about my mother's death, but as I looked at the bowed heads and somber faces of my family, I knew the question remained in their minds as it did in mine. *Was her death more than an accident?*

CHAPTER 12
THE FACE OF TERROR

My mother had as many faces as she had alters. She had the face of an upstanding and moral housewife. This was the face she paraded around the neighbors and at church. She also had the face of a kind and loving mother. However, she had other faces that were terrible: the face of a drug addict and the face of a monster. Those were the faces we feared the most. Though they weren't always in sight, they were ever present behind my mother's eyes, like a lurking fog in the horizon.

I was sixteen when I first confronted my mother about her drug problem. It was a problem that came and went but became progressively worse. Her episodes seemed to increase as the drug abuse did. It is uncertain whether the increase in episodes was due to the increase in drug abuse or the other way around. Either way, it took a heavy toll on our family.

We had dealt with my mother's "reactions," as she called them, since we were young children. She would often be disoriented and in some cases would completely pass out. She told us it was due to a reaction with the medications the doctors had given her, and once the doctors figured out the right dosages, she would be fine. We believed that as a family, but as our youth passed, so did our trust in adults. In high school, I became more aware of drug abuse and the signs of it. I began to notice similar signs in my mother, but when I confronted her about it, she denied it. Even my family denied it.

In desperation, I began recording the number of times she took her medications. Soon it became undeniable that there was a problem.

"You have a drug problem, Mom," I said.

My mother scowled at me. "How dare you accuse me of that," she said. "Those medications were prescribed by a doctor. I am not like Brenda."

Brenda was Mom's adopted sister. She had experienced the same abuse by their father as my mother had. Unlike my mother, however, Brenda did not keep it inside. She acted out. She had been in jail several times, had children from several different men she did not know, and was a crack addict. Mom often cared for her children while she served prison sentences.

In my mother's eyes, she was completely different from Brenda. While my mother felt shame for what my grandfather did to them, Brenda used it to extort favors from him. It was difficult for Mom to accept that her drug addiction was just as serious as that of Brenda's.

"I'm not saying you're like Brenda," I said, "but you do have a problem."

"I don't have a problem. I take those medications because the doctor prescribed them."

"Mom, you are taking more than you're supposed to."

"I am not."

"Yes, you are."

"You don't know what you're saying, and I'm done talking about it." She stormed into the kitchen and began making herself busy.

I followed her with my notebook in hand. "I have proof that you have been taking too much medication."

"What proof?"

"I kept a record of each time you took your medication." I opened the notebook and handed it to her. "See. You've been taking more than what it says on the bottle."

She looked at the notebook and then at me.

"You were spying on me?" she said. Her voice was thick with rage. She took the notebook and began tearing pages out and throwing them away. "This is my house," she said as she tore another page, "and I will not be spied on in my own house." Her tearing became even more violent. "How dare you!"

I tried to stop her from destroying the notebook, but she pushed me against the wall. The force was more than I had expected from my mother. She was such a frail woman that I was astonished by her ferocity. "Mom, stop," I said.

She threw the notebook in the trash with the shredded pages and then walked toward me, stopping short of my face. Her face was different than I had ever seen it. It was the face of pure hatred, and when she spoke it was gruff and intimidating. It was no longer my mother. "If you ever spy on me again," she said, "you will wish you hadn't."

It wasn't the simple threat of an angry parent. It was real.

She took a box from the cabinet and with one fell swoop of her arm managed to empty the entire shelf of medication into it. She then stormed off to the bedroom, slamming the door behind her. The force jolted the entire house.

I remained against the wall, my chest pounding. I had seen my mother angry, but never like that.

Blain walked into the kitchen. "What are you doing?" he said. "You can't accuse Mom of being a druggie. That's serious."

"I have proof, Blain." I walked over to the garbage and retrieved what was left of my notebook.

"I don't believe it," he said. "Those reactions are because the doctors haven't gotten her dosages right. It's their fault, not hers."

"Don't be naive," I said. "You know as well as I do it's not the doctors. She has prescriptions in our names that she's been taking."

"You're lying."

"No, Blain. I'm about the only one around here who isn't."

"Why do you hate her?"

The question hit me hard. "I—I don't hate her." I picked up the rest of the pages. "I just want her to stop."

"You want her to be normal," he said.

I said nothing. I walked past my brother and up to my room.

Seeing the futility in confronting my mother, I decided to talk to my father. I thought that if he knew, he would stop it. I was hesitant at first; Dad had already threatened to leave Mom, and I was afraid he might do it if he knew she was abusing drugs. Though my father was absent most of the time, my greatest fear was that he would leave us alone with Mom. With Dad around, at least I felt secure in knowing there was at least one adult I could turn to for help. I could not let Mom's addiction continue. I had to tell him. Something had to be done, and I didn't think I could do it alone.

Dad was resting on the recliner as he often did after work.

"Dad," I said, "can I talk to you?"

"Sure, Honey," he said. He raised the incline and sat up. "What do you need?"

"It's about Mom," I said.

He sighed. "Tiffany . . ."

"It's important," I said.

"What is it?" he asked.

"I have been recording how much medication Mom's been taking," I said.

"You've what?" He raised himself up. "You should not have done that," he said. Your mother deserves her privacy and . . ."

"I had to."

"What do you mean you had to?"

"She's been abusing her medication. Someone had to do something."

"Are you saying she's a drug addict?"

I hesitated. Even now, I did not want to say it, but there was no denying it. "She is addicted to prescription drugs."

"I can't believe you would say that about your own mother," he said. "It's disrespectful. You should be ashamed." He turned away, grabbing the remote and flipping on the television, a signal that the discussion was over.

"But Dad . . ."

"I don't want to hear it," he demanded.

"Why won't you listen to me?"

"I don't want to talk about it."

"It seems nobody does," I said. I was frustrated by the apathy my family was showing. "You think you can ignore this and it will go away, but you can't. Something has to be done before it gets any worse. How can you not see that?"

He turned to me. "There is nothing wrong with your mother."

"There's everything wrong with Mom, and you know it."

"Don't talk about your mother that way."

"Why not?"

"You should respect your mother and mind your own business."

"How am I supposed to respect her when she's lying to all of us?"

"Your mother is not a liar."

"Then what do you call it?"

My father had little patience with anything that did not have to do with cars, and one thing he had absolutely no patience for was anything that had to do with my mother. He glared at me while squeezing the remote in his hand, his knuckles white from the intensity of his grip. "Go to your room," he said.

"But . . ."

He gritted his teeth. "Go to your room."

My father was not physically abusive to any of us, but his temper would on occasion get away from him. In those cases, he sometimes hurt someone, not intentionally, but inevitably. As children we knew when to back away.

I ran out of the room, tears clinging to the edges of my eyes.

I was alone. No one wanted to admit that Mom had a problem despite the truth that was so obvious. She was ruining the entire family and no one cared. I did not know what to do but cry and write what I felt. I hated my mother for what she was doing and for the lies she continued to tell. *How could she?*

Over the next few months, I did manage to convince Lydia of Mom's problem. She had been suspecting it for a long time but did not want to say anything. Lydia had been sick for many years, and Mom continually took her to the doctors. Despite Lydia's insistence that the pain was fine, Mom convinced the doctor to write her prescriptions for it. Lydia did not take any of the medication, and yet she often found empty pill bottles with her name on them in Mom's room. After that, she knew that Mom was abusing prescription drugs, but like me, she didn't know what she could do to stop it.

Since confronting Mom only made things worse, we decided to take another approach. Together we decided to find Mom's stashes of medication and hide them from her. We hoped this would at least limit the amount of abuse. We thought if nothing else, it would confirm to the rest of the family that she had a problem.

"Where are they?" Mom said. She frantically tossed up piles of newspapers that were cluttering the dining room table. "I left them right here on the table."

I smirked, reading my book on the couch. I was watching her display as she frantically hunted for her pills. She was like a wild animal in desperate search for food.

"Have you seen them, Tiffany?" she asked.

"Seen what, Mom?" I hid my amusement behind the pages of my book.

"My medication," she said.

"What medication?"

"The one the doctor gave me for my neck pain," she said. She overturned a chair and began rummaging around the floor on all fours under the table.

"You seem okay to me," I said.

Mom poked her head from under the table. "What is that supposed to mean?" she asked.

"I mean you don't seem to be in that much pain," I said. I couldn't help but smile.

"What would you know about pain?" she said. She stood up and walked to the kitchen. I could hear her ruffling through papers and boxes.

"They're not on the counter, either," she said. "Are you sure you haven't seen them?"

"No," I said. I hated lying to her, but I couldn't let her have them.

She walked out of the kitchen and watched me for a few minutes as if trying to discern whether I was telling the truth.

"You haven't done something to them, have you?" she asked.

I said nothing, burrowing deeper into my book.

"Tiffany, tell me the truth. Have you done something with my pills?"

"No," I said hesitantly.

My mother walked up and grabbed the book out of my hand and flung it across the room. "Where are they?" she asked. "I know you have done something with them."

"What are you talking about?"

"You know what I'm talking about. Where are my prescriptions?"

"You don't need them," I said.

"The doctor wouldn't have given them to me if he didn't think I needed them."

"The doctor doesn't know how much you're taking."

My mother shook her head. "Not this again," she said. "I am not taking too much medication."

"Then how do you explain your *reactions?*"

"That's just it. They're reactions to the medications the doctors have given me."

"Well, I don't see how you have so much faith in doctors who can't seem to get your medication right."

"They are adjusting the dosage."

"That's a lie, and you know it."

She scowled at me. "Are you calling me a liar?"

"Isn't it obvious?" I said.

My mother slapped me across the face. "Don't you ever call me a liar," she said.

I slumped down on the couch, my face stinging and wet with tears. I was shocked that my mother would slap me. It was not painful as much as it was hurtful.

Mom looked at me on the couch. She stumbled back, seeing what she had done. She walked out of the room, not saying a word.

I sat there alone on the couch not wanting to move. I could hear Mom in the distance, pulling out drawers and overturning furniture. Lydia and I had been thorough in taking my mom's medications, making sure she had not stashed any in her room. I heard more things being tossed about, only this time it was not from my mother's room, it was from mine.

I leaped from the couch and darted to my room. Mom had pulled the drawers from my dresser, spilling the contents. She was now on her knees, searching under my bed.

"What are you doing?" I exclaimed.

She looked up from the floor at me and then stood up. "Where are they?" she said. She pushed her way past me and began looking through my closet.

"They're not in here."

"Then where are they?"

"We dumped them down the toilet," I said.

She glared at me for a few moments. "You're lying," she said. "They're somewhere in this room, and I'm going to find them."

"They're not in here," I insisted.

She pulled clothes from their hangers and toppled boxes. She walked to the desk and began dumping out drawers.

"You have no right to go through my things like this," I said.

"I have every right," she said. "I'm your mother."

I pulled at her shirt, pleading for her to stop, but she simply shrugged off my pleas. With determination she upturned everything in my room in search of her pills.

"You stole them, and I am going to find them." After several minutes the room was reduced to disorganized piles scattered about the floor with no sign of her medication. Finally, she sat down on the bed. Her attempts to find the pills had been fruitless. There would be no point in searching further. "Please, Tiffany, I need that medication," she said. She began to cry. "You don't understand the pain I'm in."

"Mom, I can't." I felt guilty for not giving her the medication. What if she was in pain? However, if I gave in, she would just continue to abuse them. She would never stop. I had to make a stand whether she was in pain or not.

"You hate me, don't you?" she said in Vicki's whining voice. "That's why you're doing this."

"If I hated you, I wouldn't care if you took them," I said.

"No, if you cared about me, you would know how much pain I was in."

"Mom, if you cared about this family, you would see what your drug addiction is doing to us."

"You want me gone, then," she said, "is that what you want?"

"No."

"You wish you didn't know me. You wish I wasn't here."

"You know that's not true," I said. "I love you, Mom."

"I try to be good," she said. "I really try. I'm sorry I haven't been the perfect person you want me to be."

"I don't want you to be perfect," I said. "I just want you to be you, but I can't let you do this."

"No, you hate me. You wouldn't do this if you didn't hate me."

"That's not true."

"Yes, it is. You hate me."

"I don't hate you, Mom. I . . . Just stop it. Stop saying that."

"Maybe I should leave. I'd probably be better off dead."

"Don't say things like that."

"You would be better off," she said. "You all would be better off."

"No, we wouldn't. Now stop it."

"Then why won't you give me my medicine?"

Every part of me wanted to give her the medicine. I just wanted it to stop, but I couldn't. If I wanted it to stop—if I wanted her to change, I had to stop her myself. "I'm not giving you the medication."

Mom looked at me; her eyes were no longer tearful, no longer pleading. They were cold like the day she had threatened me. She stood up from the bed and in a matter of seconds crossed the room and threw me against the wall. My back struck a picture frame, sending it crashing to the floor. She moved in closer like a stalking predator, her hands jetted out, pressing against my throat.

I thrashed about trying to grab her hands away, but she seemed stronger in her state of rage.

She moved her face close to mine. "Give me the pills," she said.

"No."

"I need those pills."

"Stop it. You're hurting me."

"You can't understand the pain, but I do," she said. "She's not going to suffer anymore."

"What are you talking about?"

Her grip tightened, making it harder to breathe. I didn't want to hurt her, but she wouldn't stop. "Stop it! You're choking me," I pleaded.

"Give me the pills."

"Let go."

"I won't let you take those pills away," she said. Her nails dug into the side of my neck. I was no longer her daughter, and she was no longer my mother.

"I'll kill you before I let you hurt her," she said.

"You're not making any sense."

"Give me the pills," she screamed.

She wasn't going to stop. I grabbed her small frame and threw her back as hard as I could. As ferocious as she may have been, it was not hard to push her away. In body, at least, she was still Mom. She toppled backward and fell to the ground. I was concerned I might have seriously hurt her but was too afraid to find out. Before she could get up, I ran into the bathroom and locked the door.

On the other side Mom began pounding. "Open this door," she yelled. She pounded hard, putting her full weight on the door. The door barely held, the wood frame creaking and cracking with each blow. I sat against the door, bracing it with my body. The pounding came in waves with the constant shouting of obscenities and threats in between. After a long battering of the door, the pounding ceased, but I remained behind the locked door cowering in fear of what was out there.

It was not my mother, at least not the mother I knew. She had become some sort of monster. In my mind I could see her face with gnashing teeth and cold, bloodless eyes. Still, despite the horrific expression, it was Mom's face. It was Mom who had tried to strangle me, and it was Mom who had threatened to kill me. I tried to separate what I had just witnessed from the loving mother that I knew, but I couldn't.

I sat quivering, my nerves disassembled, like some piece of broken circuitry. Adrenaline pounded through my veins with each pumping of my frightened heart, causing my stomach to twist and churn to the point of wanting to vomit. I breathed heavy and hard, never stopping. My body felt out of control. I could not calm down, the vision of Mom's face continuing to pour into my thoughts, exciting my anxiety. All I could do was huddle against the corner of the door and sob uncontrollably.

I remained there for several hours on the bathroom floor, until all that could be heard was the distant chirping of birds outside. Somewhere in the house Mom had collapsed, possibly exhausted from the exertion of so much violence. She would awake as if from a dream and know nothing of what she had done, but I would always remember. That face would forever penetrate my nightmares, a terror in the night.

CHAPTER 13
NEVER TO RETURN?

"It's here," Lydia exclaimed as she walked in the door with the mail. She had been camped out in front of the mailbox impatiently anticipating a letter from our church's headquarters ever since she decided to put in her papers to serve a mission for our church.

In the LDS faith, every young man at the age of nineteen is encouraged to serve a mission for the Church. At twenty-one, young women have the same opportunity but are not encouraged as much as the men. For the women it is more of a personal choice than an actual duty. These missions are sources of strengthening and growth for members of the Church. Young men and women are transported across the globe, spending anywhere from eighteen months to two years with no contact from their families other than the weekly letters and phone calls on Mother's Day and at Christmas.

For many, a mission means an interruption of their education as they often sacrifice scholarships and other opportunities. They are far from vacations, as the regimen is grueling with more than twelve hours of work a day, six days a week, holidays included. One half day a week is appointed to take care of laundry, grocery shopping, cleaning, and the occasional sightseeing. With the amount of work needed and the long separation from family, coupled with the slammed doors, impoverished conditions, and insults that often accompany missionary work, it is a wonder that anyone goes at all. Yet most members who serve missions say it was the hardest and best two years of their life. Did I mention that the families have to pay to sustain the missionary the entire time? In many cases young men and women save from early childhood to pay for their missions. In our case, because we had very little money, the Church funded the mission with donations from various Church members.

Whether one agrees with religious proselytizing or not, missionaries of any faith have to be respected for their devotion. A mission is a matter of faith.

"I wonder where I'm going," Lydia said. Her excitement exuded from every pore of her smiling face like a brilliant sheen that covered her. It had been a long time since I had seen Lydia that happy.

"I don't know," I said. "Why don't you open it?"

"I have to wait for everyone to get here," she said.

"Hey, everyone," I yelled. "Lydia's got her mission call."

Dad shook himself from his sleep on the recliner. The once-quiet home burst with movement as siblings poured into the room. We all gathered around Lydia. Mom trailed in last, slow and reluctant. The only one missing was Tammy. She was with her fiancé, Jeremy. Her marriage announcement came with much difficulty, as she was only seventeen and her husband, Jeremy, in his early twenties. Rather than chance their elopement, my parents gave their permission for her to wed.

"Well, they're here now," I said. "Open it!"

Lydia beamed brilliantly as she tore into the large envelope. Everyone waited quietly as she read the contents. After a missionary sends in their papers to go on a mission, the Church replies with a mission call. The call comes in about three grueling weeks of waiting. Within the envelope's contents are instructions on where to report, what essentials to bring, and the most anticipated of all—the call, a formal letter addressed from the president of the Church stating the location where the mission will be served. That was the paper Lydia was reading.

"So where are you going?" Blain asked.

Missionaries do not get to choose the location of their mission. This brings the person receiving the call the most anxiety as they look forward to the call. Overseas missions were usually preferred over stateside due to the exotic nature and the chance to learn a new language and interact with a new culture.

She looked up from the envelope. "Chicago," she said.

We waited to see if there was any disappointment in her demeanor. She paused for a minute, and then tears welled in her eyes. She walked to my father and embraced him, tears streaming down his face. Chicago was where Dad served his mission.

"Well, at least it's not Idaho," Blain said.

We laughed. Each of us hugged Lydia in turn, with Mom going last. She was not thrilled to hear about Lydia going on a mission, resisting her the entire time. Mom always felt threatened by the fact that we would all someday leave. I guess somewhere inside her heart she thought we would stay with her forever. After hearing Tammy was engaged and Lydia was leaving on a mission, Mom felt the reality of our leaving. She became more withdrawn and depressed, and her "reactions" became more frequent.

I too had my reservations about Lydia leaving on a mission. With her leaving and Tammy about to be married, I would be the last to care for my mother. Blain would be there, of course, but the responsibility would be primarily mine. I felt alone and abandoned. I was happy for my sisters, but at the same time I was angry with them for leaving me. I envied them because they had done what I could not do. They had found their escape.

It had been nearly three years since Mom was diagnosed with DID, and her episodes had begun to escalate. Bill, whom I had experienced on a number of occasions before her diagnosis, became more bold and violent. Out of all of Mom's alters, he was the only one who referred to himself by name as if he wanted us to know that he was there and that he was real, a threat carried unknowingly by my mother. Bill was violent and often tried to hurt Mom by various means, the most significant of which was the drugs. In his opinion he was protecting her from the pain she had suffered, but that was a lie. It was Mom and the rest of the family who needed protection from him.

He hated anyone he saw as a threat to my mother. This included my father and siblings. Bill often made threats on our lives and continually used Dad's large, husky body as a punching bag. There were occasions when I think he may have even tried to poison us, as Vicky made us drink ipecac because she said we were given bad food. Many of these attempts were foiled by the alters who were our protectors: Julia and Vicky. They would warn us when Bill was going to come out so that we could leave. In some instances, Julia would instruct Dad to leave the house before Bill took over.

When Mom was Bill, we knew it. Her eyes were different. I could always tell by the eyes. Over time we learned to recognize the signs of Bill and avoided Mom whenever he came out. Most of the time, he would sit in the living room, swearing and brooding. Though I refer to Mom in these episodes when Bill was out as "he," it was still my mother's body. Her mannerisms, however, reflected that of an angry and violent man—a man capable of killing, trapped in a fragile woman's frame.

"I won't let you leave," Mom yelled at Lydia a couple of weeks from the date of her mission departure.

"I'm going on a mission, and there's nothing you can do about that," Lydia said.

"If you leave this house, you better never come back," Mom said.

"Then I won't come back, but I'm going on a mission."

I stood in the kitchen listening to the exchange. There had been several such exchanges since Lydia got her mission call. I had joined in on some of them, coming to Lydia's defense, but today I didn't have the energy to argue anymore. I felt bad for Lydia and wished Mom could just accept that she was going to be leaving. I wished she could be happy for Lydia, but the truth was I had a hard time accepting her departure myself.

"If you loved me," Mom said, "you would stay."

"Don't start into that."

"I'm your mother, and I say you can't go."

"I'm not a little girl anymore," Lydia said. "I'm an adult now, and you can't tell me what I can and can't do."

"I'll make you stay, then." My mother walked into the kitchen, Lydia following. I stood by the sink, drinking a glass of water, trying to remain unnoticed. Mom walked to the far counter, her back to us. "I would rather you were dead than leave me," she said. "I will kill myself and take you with me."

"What are you talking about?" Lydia said.

My mother turned to us with a large cutting knife in her hand.

"What are you doing?" I asked.

She didn't answer, but in her eyes the message was clear: this wasn't Mom—it was Bill. He had threatened Lydia with a knife once before, but on that occasion, Lydia had managed to wrestle Bill to the ground and hold him there until Mom passed out.

"Stop," I screamed. But it was too late.

Bill moved across the kitchen floor with the knife raised above Mom's head, yelling, "You'll never leave this house again."

Lydia ran to the bathroom and tried to close the door, but Bill was there with the knife, trying to strike at her from the crack in the door. He pushed harder on the door, forcing it open, while Lydia struggled within to keep her out.

The shock overtook me, gripping me with terror. My faculties left and instinct took over. I dropped my glass and ran after Mom. I struggled with Bill, pulling him from the door, the knife flailing like a striking serpent.

Lydia threw open the door and lunged on Mom's arm, securing the knife on the ground. While she held the arm, I pried the knife from Mom's hand. Together we lifted Mom's body. We dragged Bill kicking and screaming through the kitchen. He bit at me, causing me to lose my grasp on Mom. He pushed Lydia down and ran to the bedroom, shutting the door behind him.

I helped Lydia up. We tried to push the door open, but it would not budge. I pounded on the door. "Open up," I said. The uncertainty of what Bill could be doing in there wore on us. If he could not hurt us, he might attempt to hurt Mom.

The door opened. Lydia and I stepped back. Mom had an opened pill bottle in one hand and with the other, Bill swept a handful of pills into her mouth. We grabbed her and tried to pry her mouth open, but Bill had already swallowed them. He smiled victoriously. "I'm taking her away from you," Bill said.

We wrestled the rest of the pills from her hand and again made our way to the living room, with her flailing behind us. We sat Mom in the rocking chair, and Lydia held Bill down while I grabbed dishtowels from the kitchen to restrain him.

"I'll kill you," he yelled as we tied Mom's arms to the handles of the rocking chair. "There's nothing you can do."

We ignored his threats. After Mom was secured to the chair, we went to the kitchen and began discussing what to do with her.

I looked at the pills she had in her hand. It was Darvocet. "How many of these did she take?"

"I don't know," Lydia replied.

"We need to call the police or something," I said. It was at that moment that Dad came home.

"What is going on here?" Dad bellowed. He ran over to Mom

sitting in the rocking chair, restrained by towels tied around her arms. "What are you kids doing to your mother?"

"No, Dad," I pleaded. I pulled tightly on my father's arm. "It's Bill."

Dad paused. He turned to me, his eyes staring sternly into mine. We rarely, if ever, used the names of Mom's many alters, but Bill was an exception. When he came out, it was not Mom but something else, something terrifying. We called him Bill because that was what he called himself. "He was chasing Lydia with a knife," I said. "He threatened to kill Mom." I showed him the bottle of painkillers we had wrestled away from Bill. "I think he may have taken some."

Dad turned and knelt beside Mom. "Vickie, are you there?" Dad demanded. His voice was urgent as he gripped Mom by the arms. "Vickie, can you hear me?" There was no response.

Mom turned her head to look at Dad. Her face constricted into a scowl, and her eyes bore down on my father like hot embers escaping a fire. "Vickie doesn't want to talk to you." Bill said. Though it was my mother's voice, it carried with it a venomous sting indicative of Bill.

"Let me talk to my wife," Dad said.

"No. Vickie has suffered long enough; I am going to protect her now." Bill always claimed to be protecting Mom, but in truth he was the one who hurt her the most. "I am going to take her away from this place."

"No, you won't," Dad said. "Vickie, can you hear me? Don't listen to him." Dad was frantic now. We all were.

I began to cry. The thought of losing Mom became ever present in my mind. I began to plead with her. "Mom, don't go. You can't go."

Mom's face softened. She looked up at me, her eyes kinder now. It was definitely Mom. "I'm tired," she said. "I want to rest."

I dropped to my knees beside her and began pleading with her. "You can't leave us," I said. "You have to fight." Despite the hatred I harbored for Mom, she was still my mother. I wanted nothing more than to have her stroke my hair as she did when I was a child and tell me it was going to be okay.

"You don't understand," Mom said. "I'm tired and I don't want to fight anymore."

"What about us?" I asked. "What will we do?"

"I'm sorry. I can't . . ."

"No. I don't believe that and neither do you." I was angry now, angry that she could even contemplate leaving us. "You're our mother. Start acting like it."

Her face was filled with pain and concern for us like one seeing her child for the last time. "Good-bye, dear," she said. Then her face faded into that distant look as if she were falling into a dark abyss of nothingness.

"No!" I screamed. "Come back."

The hatred returned in her eyes. Startled and horrified, I backed away. She looked at us with a triumphant grin; it was Bill again. "Vickie's gone," he said. "She's not coming back."

Dad pulled me back. "Now you listen to me," he said to Bill. "You let me speak to my wife."

"She doesn't want to speak to you," Bill said.

"I don't believe you."

"She doesn't want to be here. She doesn't want to hurt anymore."

"You're lying," Dad exclaimed.

"I'm taking her where you can't hurt her anymore," Bill said.

"Oh no you're not," Dad said. He stood up and ran to the bedroom.

He emerged again with a vial of consecrated oil. In the Mormon Church, every worthy male member has the opportunity to receive the priesthood, which means he is able to perform certain ordinances for his family such as giving blessings.

Dad stood over Mom. He dabbed some of the consecrated oil on her head and then clasped his hands over her head. He closed his eyes and began a blessing. We sat around him, our arms folded in the act of prayer. Mom scowled and gnashed at us with her teeth.

"In the name of Jesus Christ," he said. "I command you to leave." He completed the blessing, turning to my mother to see if she was still conscious. Mom's body had gone limp, and she was no longer thrashing against her restraints.

"Vickie?" he said. "Are you there?"

My mother lifted her head, her eyes calm. "She is here," she said. "She is resting."

"Who are you?" Dad asked.

"I am Veronica," Mom said.

"Where is Bill?" he asked. "Is he gone?"

"He is still here, but he is imprisoned."

"You can see him?"

"Yes," she said. "I can still see him, but he has been placed behind bars and can no longer hurt anyone. Those of us who remain will take care of Sam now.

"Sam?"

"Sam is his son," Lydia said.

"What about the pills she took?" I asked. "Will she die?"

"She did take a lot of pills, but she won't die."

"But how?"

"We all took a portion of the pills in order to save her."

"So she'll be all right?" I asked.

"Yes, but she must rest now."

Dad untied her arms and carried her to the bedroom. Lydia and I sat outside, waiting for her to wake up. When she did awaken, she had no recollection of the event. We told her about the incident with Bill, but she did not believe us. Dad felt it was better to let it rest. I don't think I would believe it myself if I hadn't witnessed it. I don't believe that Mom was possessed in any way by evil spirits, but somehow the blessing allowed Mom to put aside the alter of Bill. From that day forth we no longer feared him. He was gone, or so we thought.

Lydia went on her mission, and Tammy married Jeremy. I was left with the responsibility to care for Mom and the family. I quit college, having failed the first semester because of the long shifts I had to undertake as a manager at work. At the time, I felt it was more important that I earn the money to help out my family. That was my duty. I wished in many ways that I could have been Tammy—swept away and married, never to return—but my place was here with Mom.

CHAPTER 14
LIGHTING THE WAY

Lydia and I waited as the florist brought out samples of various bouquets that would be displayed at Mom's viewing. The viewing was tomorrow and we were making the last arrangements for the flowers to be sent to the funeral home.

"So have you written your eulogy yet?" Lydia asked.

"It's coming along," I said. The truth was, I had not been able to write down a definite word since I got the assignment. I was hoping that it would come to me in sudden bursts of inspiration in the night, but not a drop had been pushed from my brain to the page. I was as dry as a peasant's well, echoing back the same old trite things that I hated hearing at funerals.

"How is Dad going to pay for all of these flowers?" I asked, trying to change the subject.

"He's paying for everything with the life-insurance money," she said. "Just like he said he would."

"Has he heard back from the coroner yet?"

"No. Apparently Mom's case is low priority. We may not hear back for weeks."

"Then how does he know he is even going to get the money?"

"Faith?" Lydia replied.

Dad never was good with money. Most of the time he had left Mom in charge of the bills as if she would be any more responsible. Their financial philosophy was spend, spend, spend until the creditors won't let you spend any more. It was this philosophy that had ruined their credit and the credit of several of their children. Now his house was on the verge of foreclosure, and he was spending money like there wasn't a care in the world.

I began perusing the flowers in order to hide my sudden surge of frustration over Dad's predicament. I counted the different assortments of daisies then separated them by color and counted the individual petals on each. My mind was continually breaking things down into ordered systems: categories, constructs, and patterns. These I could deal with. These I could make sense of. It was the emotions of the heart that plagued me. They could never be broken down and analyzed. The complexities of emotion simply fall away into chaos. Most simply accept them as they are, a mosaic of life's experiences, but for me that was not possible.

Lydia followed. "Has Dad spoken with you about the cemetery plaque?" Lydia asked.

"You mean Mom's tombstone," I said. People always seemed to make up names to avoid using the term *tombstone*. I guess the word sounded vulgar to the ears of the mourning. It carried with it a visage of the dead rising from the ground.

"Yes, her tombstone."

"No, Dad hasn't said anything."

"I guess he wanted me to talk to you about it," Lydia said.

"About what?"

"We know how you love lighthouses," she said, "and you hated it when Mom began collecting them after you."

"No." I shook my head. "Not on her tombstone."

"I know, but it's what Dad says she would want."

"I was going to have that on my tombstone."

"You still can."

"Yes, but now every time I see one of my lighthouses I will think of Mom's tombstone," I said.

I had a large collection of lighthouses that filled the bathroom at home and spilled over into other areas of the house. I had been collecting them for several years. I had lighthouse blankets, a lighthouse shower curtain, and matching lighthouse towels. I even had lighthouse pillows on my couch. Much to my husband's chagrin, there wasn't a place in our entire house that did not have some sort of lighthouse. My dream when I was younger was to be married in an LDS temple on the coast of California that had been used as a lighthouse at one time.

It was more than an object; it was a symbol. Within their cylindrical shapes and swirling beacons was the representation of *my* life. My mother had stolen that part of my life through her imitation. She had never even seen a lighthouse until I started collecting them and begged to see a lighthouse up close on our trip to Oregon.

A lighthouse is an ensign on a hill, shining its light across the raging seas, beaconing the wayward sailor to safe waters and warning them of the rocky dangers that threaten to dash their ships to pieces and relinquish them to the murky depths of the ocean. They represent what I wanted to be, a lighthouse standing like an island in the midst of raging storms, beaming hope to those who may be lost.

Lighthouses are unique. No two have the same stripes, and lenses are specifically cut for that lighthouse. A lens from a light-house in California would not fit one from Oregon or Virginia. They are each different with their own character and history. The number of cuts on the lens determines the ability for their light to pierce through the misty darkness, reaching ships farther from the shore. In like manner, the cuts we sustain through our trials, if accepted without complaint, allow us that ability to shine more brilliantly and reach the hearts of those around us who may be struggling.

Within the symbol of the lighthouse was encased my purpose—my meaning. I did not want to share that with my mother, yet she took it from me, collecting them alongside me. I had shared with Mom this obsession when she was alive and now they, my father, wanted me to share it with her in death.

"I'm sorry," Lydia said.

"Sorry? You don't understand what lighthouses mean to me."

"They mean a lot to all of us."

"Yes, but that was my thing, and she stole it."

"She didn't steal it," she said.

"Then what do you call it?"

"Admiration."

"What are you talking about?"

"Mom always admired you," Lydia said. "She saw in you what she wanted in herself: a strong will, boldness, determination."

"I'm not strong willed," I said. I hated any accusation that I was stubborn, though I knew I was.

"What I mean is, Mom wanted to be more like you. When you started collecting lighthouses, she did too."

"Why?"

"I guess she felt she had no identity of her own."

The thought of Mom not having enough identities was sadly comical. "I know I shouldn't have hard feelings. After all, I'm an adult now, but it's just hard not to feel some of the feelings I felt growing up."

"I know," Lydia said. "I've had the same problem since Mom's death, but that's what this funeral is about—to let go of those feelings."

"But how?" I asked. I had been trying to let go of Mom my entire life; how was it possible to do it now?

"I don't know. I've been trying to let go myself. It's just something we have to do."

That was like telling someone that they had to land a plane without any directions or instruction manual. Life was just that way. We were put on this earth with nothing but our backsides to support us, and somehow we are expected to make it through.

Some have parents to fall back on, to teach them. We had the Church, but even that didn't seem enough at times. You can't exactly turn to the Bible and expect step-by-step instructions on how to deal with a mother with DID. Even dealing with death was a bit hazy. I would have to fumble my way through this like so many other things in life. I would falter and at times fall, but I would always get back up again. I guess that's all God really expects anyway.

"Come on," Lydia said. "You never depended on me for help before."

"Lydia," I said. "I always depended on you for help."

"What are you talking about?"

"Do you remember when you were first diagnosed with your disease?"

"That was a long time ago," she said.

"That was the first time I realized you might not be there for me," I said.

I was fifteen when my mother told me the news. I was sitting in my room, practicing the flute. She entered and sat next to me on the bed.

"Tiffany, I have something to tell you," Mom said.

I put down my flute. There were few times that Mom entered my room, and they were almost always urgent. "What is it?" I asked.

She placed her hand gently on my knee. I could see her mascara smudged, remnants of fresh tears. "We just got back from the doctor's," she said.

"Did they find out what's wrong with Lydia?" I asked.

"She has pseudo tumor cerebra."

"What's that?"

"It is a disease where she has too much fluid in her spinal chord, and it is putting a great deal of pressure on the back of her eyes.

"What will happen to her?"

"Well, despite debilitating back pain, she will eventually go blind, and . . ." My mother choked on her words. She placed her hand over her mouth as new tears began to fall. "She might be dying."

"What? No. That can't be. They have to be wrong." I could not believe what I had been told. I could not think of my sister dying—being gone. She had to stay. She couldn't leave me here.

Mom squeezed my shoulder. "I'm sorry, dear," she said. She stood up and left the room before erupting into more sobs.

I sat stunned, unable to think. All I could think of was why—why was this happening to us? Hadn't we suffered enough? I was embittered at the news, but somehow I could not lash out at God. I went to my knees and buried myself into the edge of the bed like a child clinging to a parent's chest, soaking up whatever comfort could be afforded.

"God," I said, "you can't take my sister away from me. I need her. I can't be here without her." I ran my closed eyes across the sheets, soaking them with my tears. "She can't be dying. I won't let you take her."

For more than an hour I knelt pouring over the bed my lamentations, trying to plead with God not to take her, and He sat silent, like a father letting his daughter bleed out her rage before consoling her. I did not want speeches or advice. I am often asked how I can believe so much in someone I can't see. In that exchange, alone in my bedroom, I may not have seen God or heard His voice, but He was there in the way that I needed Him. Comfort does not come through the languishing of words but by the silent presence of one who cares. He listened to me when I needed to be heard. That I believe. His presence was recognized in the comfort I felt.

That night I wrote in my notebook a poem entitled "Guide for Me the Way," which reflected my feelings about Lydia's illness.

Life is full of ups and downs
And halfway in-betweens
It's full of smiles and full of frowns
Please tell me what this means

At times I feel real scared inside
Trying to figure life out
Why do people have to die
And give me lots of doubt

Why must people go away
Leaving me down here
Why do I still have to stay
And fight back all the tears . . .

Why is this life full of trials
And why does it last so long
Help me go those extra miles
To get back where I belong

Life seems so unfriendly
As I fight it day to day
Please, dear Father, help me
Guide for me the way . . .

Later, after talking to Lydia about her disease, I learned that the diagnosis was not as bad as Mom had portrayed it. She always did tend to overexaggerate in the telling of what she considered to be the honest truth. Death was not imminent, and Lydia eventually learned how to live with her disease. Miraculously, she was even able to keep her sight, but I knew the time for her to leave would one day come. When the time did come, I resented her for it.

* * *

"I had to leave," Lydia said. She motioned to the florist as he came out of the back room. He had an armful of bouquets.

"These are the bouquets we have arranged for the viewing," the florist said. They were a mix of lilies, sunflowers, daisies, and roses, every type of flower that my mother and all her alters loved. It was a funeral for them just as it was for her.

"I know you had to leave, eventually," I said. "But that didn't make it any easier."

"I can't believe you resented me for going on a mission," she said.

"I resented you for leaving," I said. "I was happy for you going on a mission."

"That doesn't make sense," she said as she handed the flowers back to the florist.

"I know," I said. "Nothing seems to make sense right now."

Lydia laughed. "Those will be perfect for Mom's funeral, don't you think, Tiffany?"

"Yes, they're perfect," I said.

"Well, I guess that's all that matters, then," she said.

"There will be the same type of bouquets on the casket at the cemetery," the florist added.

"Perfect," Lydia said. She smiled brightly in appreciation of the flowers.

"Will that be all?" the florist asked.

"Yes, that will be everything. Do you have the address?"

"Yes, they will be sent tomorrow."

"Thank you," Lydia said.

"My pleasure."

We stepped out of the floral shop into the parking lot.

"Do you know why I had to leave?" Lydia asked.

"To preach the gospel of Jesus Christ," I said.

"Yes, that. But that's not what I am talking about. I had to go on a mission because if I didn't go, I may have never left Mom. It was my way of letting go."

"Couldn't you have waited a few years?" I asked.

She smiled. "Do you remember what I sent you from my mission?"

"A lighthouse," I said

"Your first."

"I know."

"I sent you that lighthouse to give you hope," Lydia said. "I wanted you to see that there was more out there than what we were going through at home."

"It did," I said. "You were the reason why I served a mission, and without that I don't know that I would have ever stopped hating Mom. I read your letters, and although you never pressured me, I could always feel how truly happy you were, and I wanted to experience that same happiness. You're the reason I left."

"I wasn't the reason," she said. "I just showed you how to leave."

"So can you show me how to let go?" I asked.

"I have troubles with that myself, but I'm sure you'll find your own way. We all do."

We embraced. "So how about it?" Lydia asked.

"About what?"

"The lighthouse on Mom's tombstone."

"Go ahead," I said. "Far be it for me to deny a dying woman's last request."

"I don't know why she would choose to emulate you," Lydia said. She smiled.

"What is that supposed to mean?" I smiled too.

"Oh, I almost forgot," Lydia said. "We're meeting tomorrow morning at nine for Mom's dressing."

"Great," I said. "Can't wait." I waved as she stepped into her car and drove away.

I stood watching the cars pass on the street, wondering if I would be able to face my mother again. Another line from my poem came back to my mind: "Teach me how to love and learn the way You want me to."

CHAPTER 15
CROSSING BRIDGES

The choice to serve a proselytizing mission is a difficult one. To suspend your life for a year and a half to two years is a large commitment, one not taken lightly. But once the commitment is made, there is no looking back. Otherwise, homesickness sets in, and the days become unbearable. At the age of twenty-one, I sent in my papers to serve a Church mission and was called to the Independence, Missouri, area. I worked at the Church historic site at the visitors' center in Independence, and on occasions when I wasn't giving tours, I was able to do a little proselytizing.

"It's your turn," Sister Baadsgaard, my companion, said to me as we approached a stranger's door. "Are you ready for this?" I was a new arrival in the mission field, a "greenie" as we called them, and was working up the courage to approach people.

We were knocking on doors in the area, and while it wasn't the most effective way of meeting people, we sometimes resorted to it. We often had doors slammed in our face, but most of the time people were pleasant. In Independence, the Church is far from an oddity. With more than a dozen break-offs of the Church in the area, it was common to find people who were already familiar with the Latter-day Saints.

We were standing at the doorstep of a small house in a poorer part of town. The yard was unkempt and the grass had yellowed in parts, a sign of extreme neglect in an area so lush and green. I rang the doorbell, and we waited as a young girl answered the door. She was in her teen years, timid but courteous. I began discussing some of the teachings of the Church, stumbling nervously over my words. The young girl looked hesitantly at us.

"My name is Sister Young," I said, trying a different approach. "What's your name?"

"Sarah," she said.

"Sarah, are your parents available?" I asked.

The young girl, who stood partially in the doorway, looked over her shoulder. "Show them in," a voice said inside.

"My—my mother says you can come in," Sarah said. She opened the door wider and showed us inside.

The interior of the house was as unkempt as the outside. There were unwashed dishes stacked on the counter in the kitchen. Flies swarmed around them like huge masses of clouds. Every corner was packed with useless items that seemed to squeeze the life out of the room. A very large woman sat reclined on the couch in a Hawaiian muumuu. She had a fan next to her blowing air across her sweaty body while she sipped from a large glass of iced tea, oblivious to the disastrous state of her home.

"Well," she said to her daughter, "clear them a spot to sit."

There were two couches and a recliner in the room, all covered in laundry, food-caked dishes, or newspapers. Sarah hurried about, trying to make them suitable for sitting. As she passed by with her arms full of dirty laundry and newspapers, she looked horrified and embarrassed to have people see the state of the house. She disappeared into the kitchen.

"Go ahead and have a seat," the woman said. "Can I offer you an ice tea?"

"No, thank you," I said. My companion squirmed uneasily in her seat, not wanting to touch the filthy cushions that lay around her. It bothered me too.

"Nonsense," the woman said. She hollered to her daughter, "Get these girls some ice tea."

"No, really, we can't," I said.

"What do you mean you can't?"

"We don't drink tea."

"Oh." She paused a moment. "Make it water," she yelled.

A few moments later, Sarah walked out with two glasses of water. The glasses were smudged, and small particles floated in the water. My companion and I looked at our glasses with a slight cringe. We held the glasses on our laps. Sarah looked at us with an apologetic expression.

"Hot day to be knocking on doors, don't you think?" the woman said.

"It's not that bad," Sister Baadsgaard said. There was a slight pause. My companion stared expectantly at me.

"Pardon me," I said. "Let me introduce ourselves. I'm Sister Young, and this is my companion, Sister Baadsgaard." I leaned across and shook the woman's hand.

"I'm Muriel," she said.

"Nice to meet you," my companion said.

"You're Mormons, right?" Muriel asked.

"Yes," I said.

"From Utah?"

"Actually, yes, we happen to be from Utah, but not all Mormons are from Utah."

"So what you got for me?"

My companion and I continued our discussion of the Church. We talked about families mostly. That was our main focus. Muriel talked of her husband and the other children who weren't there. We spoke of our families too. As always, I tried to highlight the best parts of my family. I didn't mention Mom's DID or that she tried to kill my sister with a carving knife. It wasn't expected. It wasn't appropriate.

Despite my unwillingness to talk candidly of my family, it was difficult not to think of them. I sat looking at the disarray that lay before me wondering if this was how others saw my family. I saw Sarah, tearfully apologetic as if it was her fault the house was a mess—as if there were more she could have done to lessen our discomfort. I had to leave that place, not because of the discomfort, but because of what it reminded me of.

We set up another visit and said our good-byes. As we walked back to the visitors' center, my companion commented, "I feel so sorry for them. How can they live like that?"

"Like what?" I asked.

"In that mess," she said. It was as if she were attacking me.

"Maybe she has no choice. Maybe she doesn't know any better."

"How can you not know?"

"It's difficult taking care of an entire house when you're only a child," I said.

"I wasn't talking about the girl," Sister Baadsgaard said. "I was talking about the mother." She gave me a strange look. "It is sad that the problem with her weight is affecting every other aspect of her life."

"It is sad."

"I know, we could go over there and clean up for them," she said. "It could be part of our service hours."

"Maybe," I said. I thought about how I would feel having someone else come into my home and clean it. It was a wonderful gesture, but the humiliation of having to see others, complete strangers no less, clean your messes would be terrible. At the same time, it would have been a tremendous help.

"I can't wait to check the mail," Sister Baadsgaard said. "My mother is supposed to be sending a package of goodies."

"That will be fun," I said half-heartedly.

"I'll share them with you."

I smiled. "Thank you."

Including my time at the Missionary Training Center, I had been out nearly three months and hadn't received a single letter from my parents. I had no idea what was going on at home, and I had no way of contacting them without breaking mission rules. We were only supposed to call home on special holidays or in emergencies. The rule wasn't intended to be cruel; experience had shown that it was easier for missionaries if they limited their contact with home. Those who did not respect the rule fell into deep depressions of homesickness, making them completely dysfunctional. Usually, they went home.

When I went on my mission, I intended to leave my family behind and commit to the work, but as the days waned on and no word had come from home, it was difficult not to think about them. I'd spent my entire life taking care of Mom and being responsible for the family. Now my sisters and I were gone.

Why wouldn't they write me? The obvious answer was that they were neglectful in writing letters, as they were neglectful in most things. However, I continued to have that uncertainty that there was something wrong. Mom could be in the hospital. Was Blain taking care of Chris and Heidi? Did Dad lose his job? I had been using my job as a manger to help them pay for the mortgage on the home, but now I was here. How would they get by? Did they still have a home? Dozens of uncertainties plagued me in my sleep and distracted me from my work. I couldn't go on any longer. I had to have some assurance that my family was okay.

"So, Sister Young, what can I do for you?" President Richards asked. We were sitting in his office, a simple room with the necessities: desk, chair, computer, and filing cabinet. A large map outlining the boundaries of the mission hung on the wall. Beyond the necessities were pictures and mementos from home. To be more exact, he had six pencils in a mug, five pictures, and three photographs on his desk. That was what I had managed to count before sitting down.

Like the missionaries, President and Sister Richards had been called to their position and had to leave their home and his job for three years of service. President Richards was in charge of the missionaries in the Independence Mission and looked after them like a surrogate father, addressing their temporal and spiritual needs. On occasion, he would act as a counselor, hearing out the many disputes between companions and resolving the emotional wreckage that passed through his door.

"I know it's against the rules to call home," I said, "but I haven't heard from my family since I've been here, and I'm beginning to get worried.

"They haven't written you any letters?" he asked.

"No."

"And you've written them?"

"Yes."

President Richards paused, reflecting on the dilemma. "I know it's difficult to be away from home, especially for the first time, but you have to put that behind you or you will never be able to commit to the work."

"I've tried, President, but you don't understand," I said. I was reluctant to tell him about my family. "I just need to know if they're all right."

"It seems simple enough to make a phone call home, but one phone call is not going to stop the homesickness, it will just make it worse. Maybe you should wait a little longer to see if they write a letter."

"But what if something bad has happened?"

"Nothing bad has happened," he said.

"How do you know?" I asked.

"If something bad has happened, then I'm sure they would call the mission office. They have our number."

"I'm sorry, but you don't know my family."

President Richards leaned over his desk. "I've had this same discussion with many missionaries," he said. "I am sure there is very little difference between your family and theirs. Now why don't you go back to your apartment and write a letter to your parents about your concerns."

"It won't make a difference," I said.

"Why is it so important that you make this phone call?" he asked.

"My parents are not the most responsible, and my mother . . ." I stopped. "I used to be the one to take care of her, and if I'm not there, I'm afraid something bad is going to happen."

"What bad could happen?"

I sat for a moment, not wanting to say what could happen. "She could be in the hospital or dying or something."

"Is she sick?" he asked.

"In a way," I replied.

"I don't understand."

I hesitated, looking around the room as if to avoid what I was about to say. "My mother has multiple personalities."

President Richards tipped back in his seat. He swiveled slightly to one side and stared at a picture on the wall, contemplating. A few moments of silence passed during which I counted the number of lines on his tie. He turned to me and sat up straight. "Tell me about your mother," he said.

I told him of my mother's traumatic childhood and the sexual abuse she endured at the hands of my grandfather. I explained about Mom's condition and her episodes. I explained about Bill and the drug problem. It was the first time I had discussed my family with anyone, but I felt I could trust him. He was a Church leader and bound to discretion. He was also a kind man who was willing to listen. No one had been willing to listen since my counselor in junior high. I told him everything, even my feelings toward my mother, which I had to hide away, writing them only in my notebooks.

After I was done talking, we both sat silently. President Richards was a reserved man, who thought before he spoke. If he had no answers, he did not waste your time acting like he had one. Words were sacred utterances that had to be developed before delivery. When he sat up in his chair and faced me, I knew he would have something profound to say, something that would help me with my situation.

He started out slow. "Well," he said. He sighed. "It sounds to me that your mother was your savior."

I was stunned. Did I hear him right? *My mother was my savior?* There was nothing more absurd that could be said. The very thought of comparing what my mother did for me to that of some pristine individual, even Jesus, seemed sacrilegious. How could he say that? My mother was no savior.

"I don't understand," I said.

"Well, a savior is anyone that takes up the cause of aiding another in ways that are far beyond the common. Jesus Christ was *the* Savior of mankind. He gave his life to save us from sin. Others are a savior to a lesser degree, saving us from other ills that we face in life."

"I know what a savior is," I said, "but how could you call my mother a savior. Didn't you hear what I just told you? She made my life and the life of my family miserable. I hate her."

"Sister Young," he said, "I know it seems that way. She hurt you and your family. But you have to understand all that you suffered was only a fraction of what she had to endure. I have no doubt that your childhood memories are difficult, but they are nothing compared to the memories that your mother has had to endure."

"I know she suffered a lot, but she could have stopped it," I said. "She could have made it so we didn't have to suffer."

"It's not that easy." He pursed his lips thoughtfully. "Were you ever sexually abused?"

"No."

"Sexual abuse is usually a cycle that continues through many generations," he said. "Was your grandfather sexually abused?"

"Yes." From what I know of my grandfather's early life, it was as unpleasant as my mother's. His father left when he was young, and his mother brought home several men, each with their own depravities. Many abused my grandfather and his siblings both physically and sexually while his mother stood by and watched.

"Do you see? It was a cycle. I imagine that your great-grandmother even went through her own unspeakable experiences. These experiences change us, either making us helpless accomplices to further abuse or worse, abusers ourselves. When someone is able to come along and make a stand against these things, it is a remarkable thing. Your mother stood against a lifetime of terrible things and, yes, she faltered, but she saved you from it."

My mother had always been the source of so much contention in my life it was difficult to see what efforts she made on my behalf. I saw what the world saw, a woman damaged and broken. I refused to see beyond these obvious flaws to the heart of the woman that lay beneath, the heart that had so graciously given love where hatred and spite would have been well deserved. She fought against incomprehensible tortures in trying to maintain what little sanity she could, like grabbing at sand steadily slipping through her hands until none remained.

Though she had every reason to turn her back on her father, she didn't. When he was put on oxygen and needed extra care, she willingly provided it to a man who had destroyed her life. I had seen her devotion as a weakness of her character, an unwillingness to escape her past. The truth was that she had escaped her past by forgiving her father. When she returned to her father, it was out of duty—not to him but to her own expression of love.

She chose to love where hatred would have been so much easier, and she found her strength in that. Though fate cruelly fractured her mind, she tried her best to be a mother to us.

"What do I do?" I asked.

President Richards clasped his hands and smiled. "I want you to imagine yourself standing on a bridge. It is an old bridge that is in desperate need of renewing, but in spite of this, it continues to hold. I want you to imagine standing on the security of that bridge, overlooking the raging water that lies beneath you. If even one support of that bridge slips, you would be washed away in those angry rapids, but they hold. And though it creaks at times, it will continue to hold for a very long time because that is what it was intended to do."

"What does that have to do with my mother?" I asked.

"Your mother is that bridge to you. She kept you from washing away into that cycle of abuse that pervaded her life. Though she had failed you in some ways as a mother, she had kept her supports strong, never losing her resolve in protecting you from that life she had known. And because your mother broke the cycle of abuse, your childhood was better than hers, and your children's childhood will be better than yours, and the cycle will continue to heal. So now it's your turn."

"What do you mean *my turn*?"

"You must be a bridge to your children, bridging that final gap to break this cycle that has been perpetuated for generations," he said.

"I don't know how to do that," I said.

"First thing we need to do is to keep you from going back to that situation at home."

"But I have to take care of my mother," I objected.

"No, you don't. She is not your responsibility," he said. "You can't take care of anyone until you take care of yourself."

"Where will I go?"

"You want to attend college, don't you?"

"Yes."

"Well, I know a nice little college in Idaho called Ricks," he said.

"I can't go away to college." Although the prospect of going away to college brought relief, there remained a part of me that was unwilling to let go. I had to cling to this world I had wrapped myself in. To lose it would be to lose who I was. "No, there's just no way. I can't afford it. I can't . . ."

"Let me worry about that," he said. "When you're done here, we'll see about getting you a scholarship."

"Thank you," I said. In all my life, no one had been so willing to help me like President Richards. I could not express the gratitude I felt. Where most looked on not knowing how to help, he listened and did what he could, opening my eyes to a greater understanding of myself and my mother. Still, there were reservations—things in myself that I could not let go of. "I don't feel like I deserve it," I said.

"What do you mean?"

"I have spent my entire life hating my mother, and even now I can't help but feel anger toward her."

President Richards smiled. "A few words are not going to change how you feel inside," he said, "but hopefully I have been able to put things in perspective. It will take a long time for you to be able to face your mother and see her the way she truly is."

"What if my mother doesn't change?" I asked. "How can I learn to love her?"

"Your mother probably won't change. You shouldn't expect it."

"Then how will anything ever be different?"

"Things will be different because you will be different," he said. "It's been my experience that the greatest change needed in this world is our own way of looking at it."

"I don't know if I can do it."

"You can, Sister Young. Save a little bit of that faith you have in God for yourself. With as much faith as you have in Him, He has more invested in you. Just trust yourself."

"Thank you."

"I think you can make that phone call now," he said. He directed me out of his office and instructed one of his assistants to allow me the use of his phone. I don't remember much of the conversation with my family; it wasn't what I needed, and President Richards knew that.

I completed my mission, returning home only briefly before going away to Ricks. There was some resistance from my mother, but in the end she conceded to let me go. In a way I had found my escape, but not in the way I had expected. Escape is more than just leaving a place; sometimes it is the acknowledgment that we can leave. President Richards had given me that.

Note: "President Richards" is a pseudonym for my mission president in order to respect his privacy, and I thank him for his kindness in allowing me to share this story.

CHAPTER 16
MASK OF PERFECTION

Though President Richards's words had altered the way I saw my mother, the changes that would come from that revelation would take many years to set in. For the most part, I avoided my mother rather than face the hard reality of how I felt about her. It is easy to love from a distance and quite another thing to love the person when they are right in front of you. All blemishes and imperfections are blurred and forgiven from a distance. So it was with my mother. As long as I was at college and she was several hundred miles away at home, I could love and forgive her. However, I dared not put that love to the test by reintroducing her into my life, but as always, God had other plans.

My first full year at Ricks consisted of a heavy load of classes, school activities, church callings, a part-time job at the nursing department, and a full-time job as a resident assistant for my apartment complex. Having given up my responsibilities at home, I adopted a whole new assortment of responsibilities. One favor turned into two, then three, until there was no end to them. Though the strain was getting to me, I could not slow down. Pausing even a moment, my mind would wander back to my home life. I had run from the darkness only to keep running, not knowing where I was going—only knowing that I had to run.

* * *

"Thank you so much for all you are doing with Mother's Week," Joni said as she brushed back her hair. She looked as exhausted as I felt.

"Always willing to help," I said. I strained to muster an enthusiastic smile.

Joni was student body officer over women at Ricks, and I was one of ten women who sat on her executive council. Each executive had their assignment and a group of women to help them fulfill that assignment. I was in charge of speakers for the year. Our executive committee was also in charge of Mother's Week at Ricks, a celebration of the mother-child relationship. Despite all my attempts not to face my mother, it was fitting that I would sit on a council that would plan activities for all the students and their mothers to enjoy together. God has a way of always making us face those things that we try so hard to avoid. Had I known about Mother's Week in the beginning, I might have said no to the executive position, but then again, I couldn't say no to anything.

"It's going to be exciting," Joni said. "We've got some great presenters coming."

"I hope it will be fun for everyone."

"I'm just so interested in meeting your mother."

"My mother?"

"Yes. You are going to invite her, aren't you?"

I paused, having no real reply.

"She must be a wonderful woman. I mean look at you. And the way you talk about your sisters."

I hadn't really told Joni or anyone about my family, especially not about my mother. Like an artisan, I sorted through my past, only divulging a handful of anecdotes and memories, so as to present a picture of perfection. Who I was to the world, to those at Ricks, was a finely constructed mosaic of partial truths, the divulgence of only the portion of me that would be looked upon favorably. Such facades were hard to maintain. Inviting my mother to come to this new life I had made would be like taking a sledgehammer to all of it. The image of my mother crashing into my life again ran through my head, paralyzing me.

"Are you okay?" Joni asked. Her face turned to a look of concern. "Working on this Mother's Week has been intense. Do you need some extra help? I can pull from one of the other committees."

I quickly shook my thoughts away. "No. No, I'm fine. Just a lot on my mind. That's all."

"Are you sure?"

"Yes. I can handle it," I said. I had said those words many times over the years, and each time their resolve seemed to weaken. "Really, I can handle it," I repeated. It was for my own convincing, not Joni's.

"You are perfectly amazing," Joni said. "You know that?"

I said nothing, only smiled.

The mornings were the biggest struggle. It seemed that each one brought a fight with it. What started as a slump became complete apathy toward the world. There was nothing to draw me out of bed other than the guilt of letting people down. I had covered myself in a dark shroud of self denial, unwilling to allow myself even the smallest gratification. All that mattered was maintaining that image of perfection I had set up for myself, and all I saw was how much I was failing to hold up that expectation. I wanted to be the way they saw me, perfect, and my every effort went to that aim. I felt that if I could maintain the illusion, then it wasn't really a lie.

As Mother's Week drew closer, the darkness seemed to surround me until there was no place to run. Like a cornered animal, I fought to survive, but my body had already given in. Every muscle ached, and my mind had become a muddled mess, unwilling to focus. After a visit to the doctor, I was diagnosed with physical depression and was urged to take it easy and maybe talk to someone.

Life is full of transformations, like transcending from one plane of existence to another. Death and rebirth. However, no change comes without those darkest moments when fears culminate. It is our fears that keep us from crossing that threshold of change. Only when things seem the darkest and we can no longer stay where we are can we make the decision to submit ourselves to change. This is a type of death. This was mine. I could not keep running from the darkness, and I could not make the next step on my own. I needed help. It was that realization that led me to the counselor's office again, this time on my own accord.

"So what can I help you with?" the counselor asked. He sat at the side of his desk in a striped sweater, the kind that young children give and their fathers obligingly wear out of love. He scratched his prickly gray stubble, waiting for a response.

I sat across from him, gathering my thoughts. At that point my thoughts did not come easy; they were swept in a torrent of confusion. Trying to avoid the silence, I started into a long explanation of my symptoms, only to be cut off.

"I'm not a physician," the counselor said. "I don't treat physical symptoms."

"But don't you want to know what's going on in my head?"

He sighed. "We'll get to that," he said. Leaning forward in his chair, he pointed to my chest. "Right now I want to know what's going on in there."

"My heart?"

"Yes, your heart," he said gruffly. "What are you feeling?"

"Tired, I guess."

The counselor said nothing.

"I don't know. I am just completely exhausted."

"So get some sleep," he replied.

My emotions stirred inside of me. So far this counseling session was not going the way I had pictured it. In my mind I had already mapped out what I was going to say and what his responses would be as if it were a script. Now the script wasn't being followed, and it infuriated me. "I'm a little overwhelmed, all right."

"What do you mean, overwhelmed?" he asked.

"I just have a lot of things on my plate. I have seventeen credit hours, I'm an RA, I'm on the executive women's council, I work, and I volunteer teaching French at a local school and—"

"That's your fault," the counselor interrupted.

The words ran across me like a cold bath. "My fault?"

"You chose to do those things." The counselor stared at me, his face stern. "Didn't you?"

"Yes, but—"

"But what? Did anyone force you to do them?"

"No, but—"

"Look, if you're overwhelmed, stop doing so much."

I could not believe that he would be so uncaring. Here I had come for help with my situation, and all I received was more guilt. Anger welled within me. "Maybe this isn't right for me," I said. "I can handle this on my own."

"Do you really feel that way?" he asked, skeptical. "Look, it isn't my job to tell you what you want to hear. It's my job to tell you what you need to hear. You may not like it. So if you aren't ready for that, then maybe this isn't right for you."

It frustrated me to have the counselor talk to me that way, when what I had expected was loving words of encouragement. I began gathering my backpack, ready to leave, when the thought struck me, *where would I go*. I didn't dare discuss my life with anyone else. I refused to even tell my church leader at the time for fear that it would affect the way he saw me. There was no one else. Callous as it was, his was the only hand extended to pull me out of this place in which I'd found myself.

"Can you? Can you handle this?"

I sat for a long moment, not saying a word. Beneath my stiff-lipped silence, emotions began to boil up, overflowing into tears. "No," I said. "No, I can't. I can't handle this anymore."

The counselor reached behind him and grabbed a tissue box. Offering it to me, he said with a smile, "You're going to need these."

Placing my backpack back down, I took the tissues. "Look, I don't know what's wrong with me," I continued in between sobs. "I think I am going crazy."

"Crazy!" the counselor exclaimed. "You're not crazy. You're just stubborn, that's all."

I smiled.

The counselor clasped his hands and smiled. "Now we're getting somewhere." He leaned back and said, "Now tell me why you think you're crazy."

I told him about my life growing up and about my mother. He was only the second person in my life whom I had told. Even the counselor in junior high knew nothing about my home life. None of my siblings were willing to open up to anyone either. My sister Tammy told a youth advisor about our mother once, but she was called a liar and told she was making it up for attention. After that, we knew it was better not to tell. Or at least that's what we told ourselves. I don't know why I told him about my family; it certainly wasn't his consoling nature. Possibly, it was the opposite. He was willing to tell me the way it was without sugarcoating it, and at that time it was what I needed to hear.

"You still feel responsible for your family?" the counselor asked.

"I know that I shouldn't, but I still feel absolutely responsible for them," I replied.

The counselor shook his head. "Well, you're not. You never were. You need to learn to let them go, especially your mother."

My lips quivered as I tried to fight back another onslaught of emotion. "I . . . I can't . . ." The words came hard. I wanted to let go. I wanted to let go of all of it, but something inside me held on as though everything that was me clung to those expectations that everyone had for me.

The counselor leaned in and stared me in the eyes. "What are you afraid of?"

The darkness swarmed around me like a tide ready to swallow me whole. I fought against the fear that filled me. In my mind, all I could see was that little girl crying under the kitchen table when she learned about her grandmother's death. Alone and exposed to the world. I swallowed hard then said, "I'm scared."

To admit my fear was to admit my own vulnerability—to leave myself naked to the world. My entire life I felt like Eve in the Garden of Eden, being told by the world to hide my nakedness. I had clothed myself in this image of perfection, unwilling to admit my own nakedness. Now I had been stripped of that image and had no choice but to face it.

"I'm scared," I said. "Scared of letting people down. Scared of letting people see my family—my mother . . ." I paused a moment. "Scared of letting them see me—the me underneath the mask."

"You're afraid people will see that you're not perfect. Right?"

"I have to be—"

"No, you don't," the counselor interrupted.

"But people expect it from me," I said.

"You women are all the same," he said. "You think you can do everything and be everything for everybody and then break-down when you can't be. You go around trying to be perfect then go nuts when you find out you're not. Well, I've got news for you. No matter what you do or how well you do it, you will never ever be perfect. What do you think of that?"

"But we're told to strive for perfection, 'Be ye therefore perfect.' Isn't that how it goes?" I retorted. "It's a part of being Christian."

The counselor scoffed. "Look, perfection is more of a guide-line—a direction that we head toward. No one gets there in this life. If people were perfect, there would be no need for this life."

"Yes, but if I'm not perfect—"

"Then what? What is going to happen if you aren't perfect?"

"I'll let everyone down."

"Get used to letting people down; it's a part of being human. We are all imperfect, so we will all let each other down once in a while. There has only been one perfect person who has walked upon this earth, and that is Jesus Christ. Likewise, there is only one individual who has ever been a complete failure, and that is Satan."

"But we're told to be like Christ," I protested.

"Sure. Be like Him the best you can. Do as He did. Love as He loved. But the key there is that you're expected to be *like* Him, you're not expected to be *Him*. No one is perfect, we all lie some-where between His perfection and Satan's failure."

"I feel like I have to be perfect."

"I know," he said. "But all you're doing is maintaining the appearance of perfection. You'll never be perfect, and that's okay. No one should expect that, and if they do, it's because they don't understand what God intended."

"What did God intend? That we be tested and tried and found worthy? If that's true, doesn't He expect us to be perfect?"

"Yes, this life can be a test, but all that God really expects is that we love Him and that when we fall, we get back up and keep trying. Your mother, I'm sure, has fallen many times, but in the end none of that matters. What matters is that she kept going."

"I don't know," I said. "It seems too easy."

The counselor laughed. "It won't be that easy when I tell you what you're going to have to do."

"What can I do?" I asked.

"Since you're so good at taking responsibility for things, I have something you actually need to take responsibility for. The fact that you're overwhelmed is your fault and no one else's. If you want to get out of this depression you're in, you're going to have to make the right changes to your life. No one can do it for you."

"What sort of changes do I have to make?"

"First of all, you need to realize there is no magic solution to your predicament," the counselor said. He stared at me sternly as he continued. "The only way out is for you to take responsibility for your well being, which means you have to say no to people."

"But—"

The counselor cut me off. "No buts. It is very important for your future that you learn to say no right now. You must learn to say no, and you must learn to be okay with letting people down. If other people have a problem with it, you can refer them to me. Heaven knows they could probably use some counseling too."

I nodded my acknowledgment.

"The next thing you are going to do is to stop accepting responsibility for your family. They were never your responsibility to begin with."

"What about my mother?" I asked.

"What about her? She is your mother, yes, but your responsibility, no. She has your father to take care of her. You worry about yourself."

"So I'm just supposed to forget about her," I exclaimed.

"No, not at all," the counselor replied. "It's just that you can't be of any use to her if you feel that you have to be there for her out of duty. You'll only resent her. You need to learn to appreciate her as a mother, not as a duty."

"I don't know how."

"It's okay. You'll learn," he said. "It won't be easy. It never is. But you can do it. Look at the life your mother had. It's never easy. That's why you can't be down on yourself for not being perfect. God loves us more than you or I or anyone could ever know. Our imperfections are not going to change that. You don't have to impress God."

I would like to say that I left that counselor's office and was fine the rest of my life, but that is not the way it works. However, I did what the counselor asked. I said no for the first time in my life, and, as excruciating as it was for me to do, I let people down. I still feel guilty, and at times I'm still afraid, but I am learning, and that's what matters.

My mother came for Mother's Week, and my life did not come crashing down. We agreed that she would bring no medication with her. For those few days, she was the mother that I remembered from vague memories. We talked and laughed and did what mothers and daughters do. She even helped me make crepes for the French teacher I had let down by telling her I could no longer teach French in the elementary. By telling someone no, I was no longer overwhelmed, but I still felt guilty. In life we have to take our baby steps. That was mine. What mattered was that for the first time, I felt I could really appreciate my mother as a mother.

CHAPTER 17
GOOD-BYE KISS

I slept very little the night before the viewing. I awoke early with Sean still slumbering beside me. My notebook lay on the nightstand next to me opened to a page of scribbles, but nothing definable. I was to meet my sisters that morning for the dressing of our mother. I had been dreading the moment of seeing Mom's dead body ever since Lydia asked me to take part. It was my duty as a daughter, but somehow that did not make it seem any better. How did my mother do it?

She had been the one to dress Grandma for her viewing. The agony of seeing a loved one in that condition seemed overwhelming, especially given the closeness she had with her mother. Now I was about to face my mother the way she had faced hers. Would I be able to do what she could not? Would I be able to let go?

"Have you seen my earrings?" I said. I was searching my vanity.

"Which earrings?" my husband asked.

"The ones I wore yesterday."

My husband looked around the room. "Are these them?" he asked. He picked up a pair of pearl earrings off the dresser.

"No," I said. Obviously he had not been paying attention to what I had been wearing. I don't know why I expected him to. What man does?

"Well, why don't you just wear these," he said.

"They don't exactly go with my dress."

"You're dressing a corpse," he said. "I think jewelry coordination is the least of her concerns."

"That corpse happens to be my mother."

"You're right, she may take offense to the pearl earrings."

"Ha ha," I said. "Do you have to mock me at a time like this?" I checked the clock. "I'm late."

He was about to make another remark, most likely about her not getting any more dead, when my fierce glare made him think twice. "You look beautiful the way you are," he said instead.

I smiled. "Thank you, but I still need my earrings."

I looked at the pearl earrings in Sean's hand. Though I had not worn the earrings since my husband gave them to me, a feeling came over me that I should wear them today. Perhaps it was the urgency of being on time. Perhaps it was something more. I grabbed the earrings and put them on. Looking in the mirror, I grimaced. They clashed terribly with the rest of my outfit. In my younger years, I would have never left looking like that, but things were different now. The little imperfections in life didn't bother me as much. I was able to accept circumstances without the need of controlling them. It was a hard lesson. One that two children and a husband, who had no concept of perfectionism, had taught me well. They knew me, warts and all, and loved me all the more for it. That is the way of love.

"I told you they looked fine," he said, glancing at my reflection in the mirror.

"No offense, but you're the last person who should be giving fashion advice."

He made a mocked hurt expression. "What are you talking about? I have great fashion sense."

"You used to wear your pajama bottoms to class at college."

"They were comfortable," he said. "Besides, you still married me."

"Don't remind me," I said. A wry smile crept from the corners of my mouth as I gave him a quick kiss, grabbed my purse, and made for the door.

The truth was, I had changed. I no longer judged the world by a harsh set of unattainable doctrines but saw it with a degree of tolerance coupled with love. Once I was able to see the world in that light, I was able to see myself in the same manner. My standards were the same. I just stopped defining myself and others by our imperfections. Instead, I tried focusing on those unique, beautiful, and precious things that make up who we are, relishing in the idea that we were all created in God's image, and God doesn't make mistakes.

I kissed Sean again, blew kisses to the kids, and walked out the door.

The funeral home's parking lot was nearly vacant, only my sisters' and the director's cars in sight. I walked to the entrance, and the director showed me into the foyer where my sisters and a few of my mom's closest friends stood. Lydia walked up to me and put her arm around my shoulder. "Are you ready for this?" she asked.

I smiled but said nothing.

We walked down the foyer to a room just off the viewing room. The director stood at the door like the guardian of a secret trove. He waited a few minutes as we composed ourselves. I did not know what I would see on the other side of the door. Would she be dressed at all? What would she look like? What would she feel like? I hadn't seen a dead body since my uncle Elmer's funeral, and I was scared.

The director opened the door and showed us in. Inside the small room was a large table covered with a white sheet. Atop the table lay my mother's body. She had her white undergarments on and a white slip, her face painted with makeup and her hair done. Light drizzled in from a small window opposite, blanketing Mom in its soft glow and giving her an angelic appearance.

I breathed slowly as I approached. The familiar stench of formaldehyde drenched my senses, bringing back memories of the encounter with Uncle Elmer. I remembered the coldness of his skin against my lips and wondered if it would be the same with my mother. I looked at her through the sunlight; her skin was tinged blue except for the places where the makeup gave her the illusion of life. I trembled with each breath, overpowered by emotion and sensory experience. I couldn't do it.

I cowered away from the body, unwilling to touch it. I did not want to see my mother like this. I backed against the wall while my sisters began dressing her.

A hand rested on my shoulder. It was one of my mother's friends, Aunt Louise we called her. She wasn't really our aunt, but after Grandma died, she filled in as a surrogate grandmother. She often took care of us when our mother was in the hospital, saving us from the less-than-adequate care of my father.

"Are you okay?" she asked.

"I can't do it," I said.

"I know it's hard, but . . ."

"I can't stand to touch her," I said. "I don't want this to be my last memory of her."

"Tiffany, it's your mother," Louise said.

"It's not my mother. It's just her body. She's no longer here."

"Yes, but it's your mother's body. It deserves the respect that your mother did in life."

"My sisters can take care of her," I said.

"But you're her daughter too."

It was always about a daughter's duty. Is suffering a daughter's duty too? After Mom married Dad, she had escaped my grandfather's abuse, but still she returned to take care of my grandmother and later my grandfather. There was a time I asked Mom why she went back home despite what my grandfather had done to her. Her response was, "He's my father, and I love him."

"But he didn't act like a father," I protested. "He was a monster."

She looked at me in that loving way she sometimes did. "That doesn't change the fact that I am still his daughter," she said.

"He doesn't deserve your love," I said.

"Who are we to say who deserves our love? We just love."

For my mother love was not something someone deserved, it was simply something you gave without question. Despite my anger and hatred, she gave it to me, something that I struggled to do for her.

"As hard as this is," Aunt Louise said, "you need to be there with your sisters. She deserves that much."

"I can't," I said. Tears erupted and I began to shake.

"Yes, you can." She embraced me, calming my shaking. Then together we walked to where my sisters were dressing Mom.

I stood next to the body, my hands still shaking hesitantly as I touched her arm. It was cold and stiff, just as I had imagined it. The formaldehyde was thick in the air, causing my stomach to churn. I wanted to run away, but somehow my feet would not move. Something kept me there despite every faculty that screamed escape. *I'm her daughter,* I thought.

I held my mother's fragile hand and stared into her face. Tears dripped steadily as I gazed at her expressionless features. Up close the illusion of her life was gone as the artificial covering of makeup could easily be seen. What lay beneath was just a hollow representation of what my memories held.

"Could you help me with the sleeves?" Lydia asked as she pulled the dress up and over Mom's chest.

I took Mom's arm and began placing it into the sleeve. It was heavy and rigid, like a mannequin. Gently, I pulled her hand through the sleeve as if any force could break it. Memories flashed through my mind, moments as a child when I would have to dress Mom with my sisters' help after she had passed out. The motions were too familiar to all of us.

After dressing her in her gown, we delicately placed her head back onto the center of the satin pillow and gently smoothed her hair. Her face was serene and pure.

Tammy placed two pairs of white socks on her feet. "She always had cold feet," Tammy said. "She told me if she died to put two pairs of socks on her feet so the mice wouldn't nibble on her toes."

I smiled. "She always hated mice."

Together we all stepped back and observed our work. Mom lay in a beautifully embroidered dress—just like the ones she admired in life but never had the money to buy.

"Something's missing," Lydia said.

She was right—something was missing. "She hasn't got any earrings," I said. "Mom would never be caught dead without earrings." The words came out before I realized what I had said. I looked at my sisters. They were holding back laughs.

"Well, we can't have her without earrings now," Tammy said.

"I didn't bring any," Heidi said. "I'm sorry, I forgot."

"Don't worry," Tammy said. "I'm sure between all of us we can spare a pair of earrings."

A moment of realization gripped me. "I have a pair of pearl earrings," I said. "Mom always wanted pearl earrings." Though I never wore pearl earrings, somehow on that day, with a bit of Sean's help, I had worn them. It was as if I was meant to give them to my mother—one last gift of appreciation to a mother I would not see again in this life.

I took the earrings out and placed them on Mom's ears. "Sorry you never got a chance to wear these while you were alive," I said. There were many things I regretted not giving Mom, things I regretted never saying. Now she was gone and those opportunities with her.

Yet, seeing her there now, she looked different. She was not the illusion of life, but the very essence of life itself. Death was the illusion that kept me from seeing what was always there. Mom was there. I could feel it. And although I could not see her, I knew she was there, and I spoke to her. "I love you, Mom," I said. "I've always loved you."

The words came from a part of my soul that had lain vacant and neglected for so many years but now came to life. I saw in Mom's face not the artificial representation of life, but the memory of a mother who loved me as well. Though I did not hear her voice, I knew she reflected the same feeling. In that moment, my heart spoke louder than any voice. It said, "I love you too, Tiffany. I will always love you."

I kissed Mom on her cheek. Though the formaldehyde remained and her flesh was cold, I was not repulsed. Memory overcame all other sensations until her body was no longer a dead thing; it was my mother alive like an eternal flame burning in my mind. I remembered laying her down to bed at night after she had fallen asleep in the rocking chair and kissing her good night. She would not move as she slumbered, simply accepting the kiss. Though she never felt it and would never remember it, I still kissed her. The kiss was for me, a tender reminder of my love for her.

Now my mother lay silent upon the table, finally at rest. As I kissed her cheek, she accepted my kiss, and I was reminded of my love for her. We were both at peace.

CHAPTER 18
LETTING GO

"Tiffany," said a voice behind the door. I was standing in the bathroom of the funeral home. Lydia stood outside the door. "Umm . . . one of your children needs a change." She paused for a moment. "Oh, and Grandpa's here."

I looked at myself in the mirror. Mascara ran in streaks down my cheeks. "Give me a minute," I said.

I pulled a paper towel from the dispenser, ran it under the water, and began wiping my black-marred face. Scenarios of various people all asking the same question ran through my mind. *How did she die?* I thought. *She died of a drug overdose, or at least that's what we suspect. The coroner hasn't really said. You see, she was abused from a small child and had a fractured psyche. The pills were just a way of escape.* I imagined their jaws dropping like drawbridges at this blunt news. It's what they suspected anyway, but somehow having a family member say it, especially at her funeral, was inappropriate.

She died on her knees praying, I would tell them. This was not a lie, and it was not an attempt to withhold some secret from the world. I loved my mother and understood her in a way that they did not. Yes, our mother had a secret, but they did not deserve to know of it until they knew her the way I did. My mother was a good woman who loved God and life despite the hardships she was presented. In all her pain, she never saw it as an excuse for her actions. Everything she did, though she may have had every right to do them, she hated. And in turn, she hated herself for doing them. The only sin my mother ever truly committed intentionally was not loving herself as much as she loved everyone else.

The fact that she died on her knees was a reflection of the desire she had to be redeemed from a life out of her control. No one can understand her feelings of absolute helplessness, subjugated first by her father and then by her own mind.

I walked with Lydia to the foyer. In the middle of a crowd of mourners was my grandfather. It was never a question whether to invite him to the funeral. We knew it was what Mom would have wanted and so we conceded. Grandpa had always been a part of our lives, but still, there was always a feeling of uneasiness when he was around. We had known from a young age that he was someone who could not be trusted; our mother had made that clear, though it was not until later that we learned what he had done to Mom.

He was a gruff man with a short temper. There was no love lost with him. If he did not like you, he made it known. He was crass and rude with no reservations about using profanity. At one time he was a formidable man, not to be messed with. Now, he carted around an oxygen tank, a shadow of the threat he once was. This made him even more irritable and prone to tantrums. He was a small, broken man of no rapport, a man who, despite his cruelty and malevolence, had been forgotten.

"Grandpa," I said with courtesy but absent of the warmth usually reserved for a loved one.

I was the only one of my mother's children who had confronted my grandfather about what he had done. In a way, he respected me for my boldness. Perhaps that is why I was often dispatched to deal with him.

"Where is he?" Grandpa asked. He hastily searched the crowd. "Who?"

"Your father," he replied.

"He's inside," I said. "What's the matter?" Grandpa's agitation was apparent.

"Your father," he said. "He did this to her."

"What are you talking about?"

Grandpa pushed me aside and made his way through the crowd and into the viewing room. Lydia and I pursued him.

Inside, he walked directly to Dad, who was talking to some relatives. "You," he said. He was brandishing his finger at my father accusingly. "You did this to her."

Dad was shocked, not knowing how to reply. He towered over Grandpa by a good foot, making my grandfather look like a small child in comparison.

"You killed her," he said, his voice lined with hostility.

"What are you talking about?" Dad asked.

"She was never happy with you," he said. "You drove her to this."

My father remained silent and composed despite my grandfather's attacks.

"She'd still be alive if it wasn't for you." Grandpa walked over to the casket. The entire room was watching his scene, and he played it like an actor, soaking up every gaze. "My poor daughter," he said. He leaned over the casket, hugging the body and crying out in sobs of grief. It was as if he was trying to make up for every terrible thing he had done to her in life.

How dare he? I thought. Of all the people in that room, he had no right to accuse anyone of Mom's death but himself. He was the cause of it all. As the crowd watched my grandfather's antics, I saw Dad slip out one of the side doors. I followed him into a darkened hallway.

Dad was sitting on a bench, his face buried in his hands.

I sat next to him and placed my arm around him. "Dad," I said, "don't listen to him. He doesn't know what he's talking about. If anyone is to blame, he is."

He sat up and looked at me, his eyes red with tears. "Maybe he's right," he said.

"You know that's not true. Mom loved you. You're the best thing that ever happened to her."

My father smiled. "Did I ever tell you about how we met?" Though my mother had told me a thousand times, I had never actually heard it from my father. "It was at a church activity at the beach. She was there with some friends. She was only eighteen." He stared off into the darkness as if imagining her standing there in all her youth. "She was beautiful," he said. "Feisty too. I was riding with another girl on the back of my motorcycle when she saw me. She decided then she wanted to be with me and nothing was going to stop her." He smiled. "She jumped into the ocean's freezing water and began flailing her arms like she was drowning. I jumped off my bike and ran into the water to save her, thinking she was crazy, but when I pulled her to the shore and saw her . . ."

Tears streamed down his face as he choked on his words. I had rarely ever seen my father cry and never so much.

"She was so beautiful," he said. "I fell in love with her immediately."

"She loved you too," I said.

"I know, and I still love her." He smiled. "Do you remember when you came to me about her drug problem?"

I still held harsh feelings toward my father for that. I felt he had abandoned us. Every time he went away to his job, I felt that way. "Yes," I said. "You didn't believe me."

"I already knew about her drug problem. Your mother begged me not to tell anyone."

"If you knew, why didn't you do something?"

"I tried. I even threatened to leave her if she didn't stop."

"Why didn't you leave her?" I asked.

"I couldn't. I loved her too much."

"Even after all she did—after her diagnosis."

"Especially after her diagnosis. She didn't ask for any of that to happen. I promised to protect her, especially after I found out what *he* had done to her." Dad motioned to the viewing room where we had just been. More tears started, and he buried his face as if ashamed.

"Wasn't it hard to keep loving her?" I asked

"Yes, but every time I thought about leaving her, I thought of that day at the beach, and I remembered who she was then. It wasn't her fault. If anyone's, it was mine."

"How can you say that?" I asked.

"I should have done something," he said. "I should have gotten her the help she needed. I should have been there more, instead of working so much."

"You had to work to provide for us."

"That wasn't the only reason I worked," he said. "I worked to get away from it."

I hesitated a moment. He had abandoned us. He'd said it himself. My bitterness rose like a tide from a swelling storm but then settled back into its place—understanding calmed the rage. "We all wanted a way out. Even Mom."

"She didn't kill herself," Dad said stiffly.

"Dad . . ."

He shook his head. "It's not like that. The coroner deemed it an accidental overdose. She had an allergic reaction to some shellfish she ate while at our anniversary dinner. The medicine she took for that on top of her other medication caused an overdose."

"So it wasn't intentional," I said.

"Not that we know of," he said. "Deep down, I don't think she could have ever taken her own life, or anyone else's for that matter. She was a mother and a wife. That kept her from abandoning us. Still I feel so guilty."

"Guilty for what?" I asked.

"That I didn't treat her better while she was alive."

"You did the best you could, given the situation. None of us are perfect. We all go wrong, but it's those ties of love that keep us together despite it all. It's what kept Mom from giving up on life, and it's what kept us from giving up on her."

"There were so many things." He pounded his fist on his knee and bit his lip as more tears made their way down his cheeks. "Things that I wanted to say to her and never got a chance to."

I put my hand gently on his as I stood. "Then let's go say them," I said. Grabbing his arm, I pulled him from the bench. Together we walked back to the casket amongst stares and whispers, like the subtle rustling of leaves to be swept away by the next gust of wind.

My father approached the casket, my hand in his. He stood, a mammoth of a man, subdued by grief. Leaning in close to her, he spoke. "Sweetheart," he said. "It's time to say good-bye." His voice was stifled by the onslaughts of emotion. "I have to stay here while you go on without me. Don't worry, though. I'll be all right. The kids will look after me like they always do." He smiled slightly through the tears. "I'll try to be good so I can see you again, my angel. We'll be together again in heaven, only I'll be better looking." He choked back a chuckle and then moved in closer. "I love you, Sweetheart," he said. "I will always love you." He kissed her for the last time.

The entire family had gathered around the casket for one last farewell. Dad nodded to Blain and Chris. They closed the casket. We huddled together and mourned for our loss as the director carted the casket away. It was time to let go.

CHAPTER 19
IN GOD'S CARE

We buried Mom near a lilac tree. She always loved the smell of lilacs in spring. Now it was all we could smell as it wafted against the breeze. The funeral service was beautiful. The program consisted of each of Mom's children sharing their good memories—just the way Mom would have wanted it. Before the funeral began, Lydia told us of a dream she had the night before.

"I saw Mom in her dress, and she spoke to me," Lydia said. "She told me that she was happy and not to be sad. She said she was free from the restraints she had in life and could now be the mother she had always wanted to be. She said she loved us and would always be with us."

My mother had been chained down by the depravity of this world. She was a hostage to her own broken and shattered mind. Despite all her efforts to be a mother, she seemed to hurt those she loved most, a tragic destiny for a woman who had so much to give. Yet she did give so much, and now she could give so much more. She was free from the life she was forced to endure, and now she could return to us whole and unblemished by the world.

Pictures of Mom smiling brilliantly were shown, and I longed for the day that I would see her again. It was more than faith—it was an assurance, one I kept close to my heart. Blain sang and played "Forever Young," Mom's favorite song, on the guitar. Heidi sang as well. She always loved to sing to Mom. Then I gave my eulogy.

The words to my mother's eulogy did not come in some flashing bolt of inspiration during the night. They came in the quiet hours of the following morning. It came in the form of a poem as so many of my feelings do, only these were not my feelings; they were those of my mother. I like to think that it was Mom sitting next to me, telling me what to write, though I couldn't see her. The poem was entitled "For Those I Dearly Love." They were my mother's last words, and I, as her mouthpiece and handmaid, delivered them to the family.

For all my family and friends
For those I dearly love
There are some words I'd like to share
As I watch you from above

First to my darling husband
Whom I cherish every day
There's so much I want to tell you
There's so much I want to say

But for now just please remember
How much I cherish you
My love for you is endless
And I'll always be with you

You called me your precious angel
From the time that you were mine
The only difference now is this
I've been given wings to fly

I'll know better how to keep you safe
And comfort your broken heart
I can prepare a place for both of us
Please let me do my part

For my whole life you cared for me
While providing your very best
It's now my turn to care for you
Please let me do the rest

I love you oh so very much
Each day I'll walk with you
And long for the day you come home to stay
When your journey in life is through . . .

Dad did manage after Mom's death. Tammy and Jeremy stayed with him for a while. It was a good distraction for him to have the grandchildren there. More than a year later he would love again and eventually marry, but my mother still resides in his heart and always will.

Her sons, Blain and Christopher, helped bear the casket to the plot. Blain gave the dedicatory prayer. He asked that she be protected, the way he had tried to protect her in life.

Now to my sons so strong and sure
And special in God's sight
I've watched you grow into great men
Both radiating light . . .

I never will forget you
And the truth you've taught to me
To always look beyond the mark
And not just what I see

To never make a judgment
Only on the outer part
But to look a little deeper
On intentions of the heart

You treated me so special
And at times I didn't see
But now I want you both to know
I know that you love me

And I love you both so very much
Don't think I've gone away
I will always be your mother
And I'll be with you each day

Each of the siblings and the grandchildren took flowers from the casket, symbolizing the things we had taken from Mom. Even though my mother had many alters, each gave something to us that changed the way we looked at life. In a way, each gave a little part of Mom that she could not give herself. Her daughters went first with husbands in hand.

Now to my precious daughters
I love you all so much
There isn't a day that will go by
Without your mother's touch

I promise I'll take care of you
And the children that you bear
You will feel my presence close
Your mother will be there

I'll strengthen you in times of need
And comfort you in trial
I'll watch your children as you sleep
And sit with you awhile

You can rest assured that I'll be there
Much stronger than before
For now I have the freedom
To give you so much more

I will always be your mother
And I'll love you endlessly
If ever you get lonely
Don't forget to call on me

I walked to the casket and took three flowers.

I took a rose for Sandy, who taught us to love ourselves no matter what. She taught us that our bodies were beautiful and that intimacy between a couple was the highest form of expression of their love. She helped me love myself despite how the world saw me.

I took a daisy for Tina, the young vibrant girl who loved the world and everything in it. Her curiosity and love for learning inspired me to go to college and pursue knowledge of the world. It also gave me the craving to travel and explore the globe, a thirst that has never been quenched.

I took a sunflower for Julie, our loving caretaker. She stroked my hair when I needed comforting and, despite my objections, showered me with strangling hugs and kisses. Most of all, she taught me to love, not by words but by actions.

There were no lilacs on the casket to take. They were Mom's favorite. Instead, they grow by her grave. When I smell their fragrance, I am reminded that my mother is still here and still has more to give.

We departed the cemetery as we had arrived, somber and quiet. For a brief moment our lives had stood still and we mourned, but now must continue on our path. Slowly, we all submerged ourselves once again into the flow of everyday life, pausing here and there to smell those fresh lilacs in spring and remember the woman who was our mother. Soon my little family would be moving to Virginia to embark on a new journey in our life, but the lilacs would always be there.

As I walked to the car, my son in hand, Cayden turned to me. "Mommy," he said, "if we move, how is Grandma going to know where to find us?"

I looked down into his innocent face. Smiling beneath a blanket of tears, I said, "She'll know. She'll know."

AFTERWORD

Despite my mother's illness and her early death, the ebb and flow of life has slowly carried us forward. My father has since remarried a wonderful woman named Cheryl, who understands where we have come from and strives to keep my mother's memory alive. Together, they have eleven children and more than twenty-five grandchildren, which keeps them very busy. Lydia is the mother of three beautiful children and is currently attending college to become a teacher, allowing her to be a role model for young people facing life's hardships. Tammy is happily married and the mother of five children. She is currently attending college to become a counselor, hoping that her own experience with adversity will allow her to be of comfort to others. Blain is a loving husband and father and spends his time playing and managing a retail sporting goods store. Christopher recently married his best friend and will be attending law school in the fall. His desire is to serve as a voice for those who are forced to remain silent. Heidi is a caring wife and a brand-new mom of an adorable baby girl. She works for the government and is just beginning her life's journey. As for me, I am the wife of a saint and the mother of five angels. I have been blessed beyond measure, and if sharing my story helps even one soul, then everything has been worth it.

RESOURCES

When I was a child, I was uneducated and unaware of the much-needed services and support that are available for anyone suffering from mental illness, sexual abuse, or drug addiction. As a result, I have collected the following information for anyone wanting to learn more, and especially for those who need help but don't know where to look. I have also added resources for anyone suffering from an addiction who is looking for hope.

nmha.org
Mental Health America is one of the largest community-based organizations associated with mental health awareness, with more than three hundred affiliates across the country. They focus on increasing awareness, making changes in policies and educating the public about the issue of mental illness. They also provide information on support groups, prescription payment assistance, finding treatment, and clinical trials.

nami.org
The National Alliance on Mental Illness (NAMI) is America's largest grassroots mental health organization. They offer information and support as well as programs for those affected by mental illness. NAMI also provides volunteer opportunities at fundraisers and other charity events across the nation.

mentalhealthlibrary.info

Run by members of The Church of Jesus Christ of Latter-day Saints, Complete Mental Health Resources' mission is to increase personal and family wellness and decrease the burdens of mental illness, addictions and emotional problems. They have resources on addiction, bipolar, schizophrenia, suicide, sexual disorders, and more.

mentalhealth.samhsa.gov

The National Mental Health Information Center is a component of the Substance Abuse and Mental Health Services Administration (SAMHSA) Health Information Network. It was established in 1992 under the direction of Congress to provide mental health and substance abuse research toward helping those who could most benefit. Their site provides information and research in various areas of mental illness.

rainn.org

Rape, Abuse, and Incest National Network (RAINN) is the nation's largest anti–sexual assault organization, providing resources for survivors of sexual assault. RAINN operates the National Sexual Assault Hotline (1-800-656-HOPE) and Online Hotline. Their site provides information, news, and inspirational stories of assault survivors.

stopitnow.org

Stop It Now is a nonprofit organization whose desire is to stop child sexual abuse through education. They educate families on recognizing the signs of child abuse and encourage adults to take responsible action if they sense a concern, before child abuse can happen.

nsvrc.org

The National Sexual Violence Resource Center was founded by the Pennsylvania Coalition Against Rape for the purpose of providing resources for victims of sexual crimes. They coordinate the national sexual assault awareness month (SAAM) campaign every April.

ndvh.org

The National Domestic Violence Hotline (1-800-799-SAFE) has an online resource to educate victims of domestic abuse and to aid them in getting relief. They are the nation's only domestic violence hotline, servicing shelters and programs across the country.

csat.samhsa.gov

The National Center for Substance Abuse Treatment is also a component of the Substance Abuse and Mental Health Services Administration (SAMHSA) Health Information Network. It promotes community-based substance abuse treatment services and provides free referrals to abusers in order to help them on their way to recovery.

For immediate help and crisis intervention involving mental illness, child abuse, sexual abuse, addiction recovery, and other crises, please refer to the following hotlines:

Mental Health Info Source: 1-800-447-4474
Information regarding mental illness: 1-800-950-NAMI
Family Support & Children's Mental Health: 1-800-628-1696
National Resource Center on Homelessness & Mental Illness: 1-800-444-7415
The national crisis helpline (24-hour): 1-800-273-TALK
Victim Center: 1-800-FYI-CALL

National sexual assault hotline: 1-800-656-HOPE

Child Help National child abuse hotline (24-hour) 1-800-4-A-CHILD

National child/sexual abuse hotline (24-hour): 1-800-25-ABUSE

National youth crisis hotline (24-hour): 1-800-442-HOPE

Adolescent crisis intervention/counseling (24-hour): 1-800-999-9999

Teen helpline: 1-800-400-0900

Youth crisis hotline: 1-800-HIT-HOME

Incest Awareness Foundation: 1-888-547-3222

Child sexual abuse hotline: 1-888-PREVENT

National domestic violence hotline (24-hour): 1-800-799-SAFE

National drug/alcohol abuse hotline (24-hour): 1-800-662-HELP

Alcohol & drug abuse helpline and treatment: 1-800-234-0420

ABOUT THE AUTHOR

Photo by Carma Gray

Tiffany Fletcher is the second oldest of six children born to a mother diagnosed with dissociative identity disorder. It was her love of writing and music that helped her cope with the difficulties of her childhood and that offered her peace amidst of chaos. To help sooth her soul, she began playing the flute in the fifth grade and still plays it whenever possible. She also taught herself to play the piano and enjoys singing any chance she gets. She knew that she would be a writer, when at the age of eight, she won her first award in her school's Young Author Fair.

Growing up in the LDS Church, at the age of twenty-one she served a church mission in Independence, Missouri, with a special assignment to serve in the Independence LDS Visitors' Center. After her mission, she attended Rick's College in Rexburg, Idaho, where she graduated with her associates degree in general studies. She went on to attend Weber State University in Ogden, Utah, where she met and married the love of her life while pursuing her BA in English. She graduated with her degree in 2004, the same year her mother died.

Mother Had a Secret is the true story of her relationship with her mentally ill mother and is the first of many books to come. She is also an accomplished poet and an aspiring children's author. In her spare time, she home-schools her children, which is both bitter and sweet, depending on the day. She currently resides in Utah with her husband, Sean, whom she absolutely adores, and her five small children whose love and laughter she can never get enough of.